Leadership Voices™

Neutralizing Bullies, Determinedly Difficult People, and Predators at Work

Linda Irby

HAMILTON BOOKS
A MEMBER OF
THE ROWMAN & LITTLEFIELD PUBLISHING GROUP
Lanham • Boulder • New York • Toronto • Oxford

Copyright © 2006 by
Hamilton Books
4501 Forbes Boulevard
Suite 200
Lanham, Maryland 20706
Hamilton Books Acquisitions Department (301) 459-3366

PO Box 317
Oxford
OX2 9RU, UK

Library of Congress Control Number: 2006925310
ISBN-13: 978-0-7618-3108-2 (paperback : alk. paper)
ISBN-10: 0-7618-3108-8 (paperback : alk. paper)

∞™ The paper used in this publication meets the minimum
requirements of American National Standard for Information
Sciences—Permanence of Paper for Printed Library Materials
ANSI Z39.48—1984

Contents

Preface

Pronouns always pose a problem for authors who wish their work to be gender neutral. For ease of reading, this work alternates between using the feminine and masculine pronouns when referring to a person whose gender is not known or when under the circumstances the person's gender is not relevant. This alternation could perhaps be confusing, but, overall, it seems easier to read than the bulky "his/her" or "his or her"; and it is more "friendly" to my editor's ears than the often used but grammatically incorrect "their."

This work addresses issues and practices that relate to both businesses and other forms of organizations. To avoid as often as possible the bulky and difficult-to-read use of slashed nouns (for example, "business/organizations" or "employee/followers") references to individual nouns ("business" and "organization" or "employees" and "followers") are alternated in a similar fashion. I hope that after a few pages this style choice will allow the text to be both understandable and easy to read and comprehend.

Finally, this work has is written with the following parameters:

1. This book is not written by a scriptural scholar. Therefore, a panel of interdenominational Christian scripture experts has assessed the portions of this work pertaining to Christian Biblical tenets about leadership aptitudes and management stewardship.
2. This book limited the comparison of sacred values and proactive management principles to those in found in the traditional American work ethic.
3. This book focuses on Christian tenets as a spiritual source. However, it is acknowledged and appreciated that other religions and "spiritual scriptures/writings/oral histories" may also be compatible with proactive management principles.

4. This book recognizes that bullies, determinedly difficult people, and predators are found in both genders, in all races and cultures, and in people professing all types of religious and/or spiritual beliefs—or lack of beliefs.

This book focuses on identifying the common voices among sacred values, proactive management principles, and your work's community consciousness. Why? Because there will always be difficult people, you at some point might even be perceived as difficult. Some differences will never be assimilated to an acceptable, collective, inclusive "new" whole. So, the term "Leadership Voices™" was derived to represent the common elements identified when leadership principles presented in Christian tenets (as practiced within the United States) are compared to proactive management principles, which in turn are the best practices to "deal with difficult people."

Acknowledgment

As the author and a steward of this book, I made a commitment to each individual contributing to this work that I would: "tend to," "care for," and "arouse" our collective energy. Each contributor demonstrated through his words and actions his commitment to congruence between his core values and actions. Each contributor's personal "story" and accomplishments refined the chaotic dissonance of energetic vibrations necessary for ferreting out just how one practically implements at work value based, proactive leadership and management techniques that deliver profits and protect us from bullies, determinedly difficult people and predators. I express my gratitude to each of the following individuals for their efficacy, wisdom, and years of support.

Joseph Beaulieu
Jeanne Brosseau
Dr. John J. Gardiner
Helen Harris
Brenden Howell
Daren Howell
Darlene Howell
Ronald Howell
Spencer Howell
Craig Irby Sr.
Craig Irby Jr.
Cardel Irby
Galvin Irby
Virginia Irby
Sandra Irby

Acknowledgement

Virginia Jackson
Jacqueline Jefferson
Natalie Leath
Ilene LeVee
Patty Nutt
Pam Pelton
Dr. Eugene Weigman
Dr. Gary Zarter

My inclusion into the consciousness that manifested this book is a humbling accomplishment and could not have been possible without my loving, nurturing, and, perceptive grandmother, mother, and father. Therefore, in loving memory, this work is dedicated to and celebrates each of their unwavering commitments to education, personal integrity, and metamorphosing spirits.

My Grandmother: The Reverend Grace Margaret Beasley Irby 1892–1995
My Mother: Grace Margaret Irby Howell, R.N. 1923–1987
My Father: Reginald Stanley Howell, M.D 1923–1999

Chapter One

Coincidence, Consciousness, Creation

Today's workforce doesn't look, think or act like the workforce of the past nor does it hold the same values, have the same experiences, or pursue the same needs and desires. The workforce has changed significantly from six perspectives: age, gender, culture, education, disabilities, and values. Shifts in attitude and values have resulted in a wider variety of lifestyles, motivations and choices.

David Jamieson and Julie O'Mara

Each of us has a Voice. Our Voice cannot be more or less than "who" and "what" we are. Paradoxically, it is our Voice that determines and sustains — or changes, "who" and "what" we are. Our Voice always creates form; you know: our visions, our future, our present, as it did our past. In other words, we cannot escape our Voice whether we are aware of "it," believe "it" manifests form, or know "it" is a perfect reflection and projection of our core values, desires, and motives. So what, specifically, is this Voice that each of us has? Our Voice is our awareness, observation, witnessing or being mindful of our mind or state-of-being (including our internal dialogue or our dialogue with another person), either spoken or written.

How often have you read or heard that a leader must have a Voice that envisions and clearly articulates his or her vision? Or perhaps you've heard that if you can conceptualize "it" you can achieve "it." These sentiments are motivational but have you ever wondered just how do you get "it," and, other than magic, how does one's Voice create form? For most of us, the practicality of these motivational sentiments is that viewing and manifesting our desires is only slightly less difficult than knowing (notice I didn't say "believing") that voice is energy and energy creates form. More often than not there is a disconnect between our Voice and our ability to:

1. specifically and clearly mentally draw the picture of what we want,
2. acknowledge that it does matter what and how we self-talk,
3. have the mental discipline to be internally congruent with our vision, our desires, and our actions; and
4. be aware that through association there is assimilation—in other words it really does matter whom we respect, associate with, and what their Voice reinforces or destroys within us.

Each of us has within ourselves the essential elements to have our Voice make each and every one of our dreams, desires, hopes, wishes, and needs manifest for us—in the perfect form that is for our highest good and for the benefit of others. Or, as Dr. Bruce Lipton's book *The Biology of Belief (2005)* so elegantly concludes as he outlines the holistic, often complex interactions between matter and energy, "You are only as powerful as your belief system."

For instance, at work and in your personal relationships have you ever conceptualized living and working in a harmonious environment that was personally affirming, shared core values, and wealth was abundant? Do you realize that all you need to start the manifestation of this vision is for you to hear your own Voice and to be open to the possibility this will occur? This first personal step, being open is—so to speak—equivalent to "ringing the doorbell" to your conscious awareness. When you finally hear the "door bell" and open the door to your conscious awareness you begin the discovery that your vision is the manifestation of precisely "who" and "what" you are. Your vision is one tangible manifestation of your energetic Voice. Your Voice is energy and energy creates form.

INSPIRATION FOR THIS BOOK

This book is the result of a two-year research project and four years of field testing the researches results.[1] The findings, the basis for this book, concluded that:

1. A Transformational Leader's voice cannot be greater than the sum of each employee's voice; leadership is a fluid consciousness that mentors, motivates, and summons the work community to produce, with excellence.
2. Transformational Leaders' spiritual or religious affiliations underscore their visions and ethics of care; apprehending their personal and collective voices, congealing collaborative consciousness, and exciting through insight.

3. Leadership Voices™ are the synchronized energetic vibrations of the work community, incorporating diverse personal core values orchestrated by proactive management principles.
4. Proactive management goes beyond honesty and sincerity, requiring discipline, balance, dominion, and congruence between core values and actions.
5. Transformational Leaders must comprehend that they, and those to whom they delegate administrative authority, create their core values in the work environment.

Field-testing took place in actual work places: both public and private, profit and non-profit, with executive management, administrators, first line supervisors: and, yes, with ordinary workfolks embroiled in dysfunctional work environments just trying to make a living. This work considers Transformational Leadership tenets, proactive management principles, and community consciousness and then examines them to consider the connections between one's core values and one's ability to quit rewarding (bully's, determinedly difficult people's, and predator's) bad behaviors and manipulative methods. You will see that by recognizing "the leader" within yourself you can model desirable behavior, mentor new followers, redirect undesirable behaviors of difficult people, and strategically defeat predators.

DEFINITION OF TERMS

Christian Tenets

Christian tenets in this study are only discussed in relationship to traditional American work ethics and leadership principles. The scope of discussion is limited to the selected philosophies of John Calvin, Max Weber, and Everett Hagen collectively viewed as (traditional) Christian business tenets practiced in the United States of America. These selected Christian tenets constitute the "traditional" American work ethic. These traditional work ethics comprise the capitalistic, traditional work ethic that expected the individual to choose his vision, work loyally and diligently on the one hand, while on the other hand, imposed total responsibility on the individual for his failure.

Community

Community is more than the sum of its parts, the individual members. The salient characteristics of true community are inclusiveness, commitment, consciousness, realism, contemplation, and spirit. A community must provide an opportunity for each person to personally contribute and be acknowledged, and must be a safe place for all individuals. A community is a group of leaders, not a group led by an individual or clique.[2]

Consciousness

Consciousness or awareness is a process of self-reflective information absorption and transduction.[3] Along with this consciousness occurs an intellectual enlightenment or illumination, which adds a state of moral exaltation, a quickening of one's moral senses, and the appreciation that one is in possession of eternal life. It is in this state that one typically perceives the world as a mystery and in this state visionaries abound.[4]

Community Consciousness

The collective reservoir of psychic possibilities, a gargantuan force aroused by awareness, intuition and appreciation, requires reflection to achieve appearance, recognition, and differentiation of form.[5]

Energy

Quantum Reality 7, which asserts that everything is made of emptiness and form is condensed emptiness, states that everything: thoughts, feelings, emotions, sensations, and associations are made of energy.[6]

Form

There is no reality in the absence of awareness/observation and awareness/observation creates reality.[7] Simply put, you, as the observer, create the subjective reality you are observing. The importance of this concept, in pragmatic terms, is that it empowers you to go beyond the passive position of witness to the active position of creator. This view provides an association between quantum consciousness theory[8] and transformational leadership principles.[9]

Integrity

Mapes (1996) states that "integrity" goes beyond honesty and sincerity, it means completeness, wholeness, or an unimpaired condition of congruence with what one says and what one does.

Leadership Voices™

"Leadership Voices™" is the term created to represent the common element identified when leadership principles presented in Christian tenets (as practiced within the United States) are compared to proactive management principles. While this project focused on Christian tenets as a spiritual source, it is acknowledged and appreciated that other religions and "spiritual scriptures/writings/oral histories" may also be compatible with proactive management principles. These synchronized energetic vibrations of a work community/team incorporates and includes diverse personal core values, collectively orchestrating proactive management principles to prosperously produce products or services.[10]

Proactive Management Principles

Proactive management goes beyond honesty and sincerity, requiring discipline, balance, dominion, and congruence between core values and actions.[11] These principles are the collection of the leader's (or those to whom administrative authority has been delegated) voice, and actions (to include: policies, procedures, laws, ethics, values, negotiated labor agreements, and other work standards) that nourish and sustain a work environment honoring diversity, stimulating productivity, encouraging excellence and aggressively supporting freedom from harassment and discrimination.[12] Competent, purposeful blending and balancing one's personal core values, actively mediating conflicting interpersonal communications and facilitating productive work systems[13] earmark proactive management principles.

Predator

An individual dedicated to using any means necessary for the consumption, and/or total annihilation, of another's spirit, dignity, and communal connection. The predator's choice of individual may be opportunistic, triggered by observed vulnerabilities, or just the response to innate periodic carnage frenzy. Predators have a compulsive need to manipulate, control, and consume—power is everything.

Sacred Values, Core Values, and Values

The basic concept(s) one has about self, representing the "I" one calls oneself. This concept represents self and all experiences of the "internal-external" world. This concept(s) organizes everything in one's life.[14]

Values, value judgments, and value systems as an abstract concept, often merely implicit, that defines, for an individual or a social unit, what ends or means to an end are desirable.[15] One's abstract concepts of worth are usually not the result of one's own valuing, but are imposed "social" products that are slowly internalized and accepted as one's own criteria of worth. In contrast, sacred values are one's core values(s), that are impregnable and inalterable, absorbed or constructed, comprising the essence of one's life, and may be quite divergent from the group's value system.[16]

Transformational Leaders

Transformational leaders are change agents and thus must comprehend that they, and those to whom they delegate administrative authority, create their core values in the work environment.[17]

Transformational Leadership

Transformational Leadership is a verb where the leaders' spiritual or religious affiliations underscore their visions and ethics of care; apprehending their personal and collective voices, congealing collaborative consciousness, and exciting through insight.[18]

Vision

Wolinsky's (1993) Level 1 wave function portrays vision as a "knowing," a "seeing," and "observation" that cultivates and integrates personal spirit and the omnipresent essence. The balancing of self with progress and the harmonizing of desire(s) with incremental developments actualizes specific, concrete, tangible achievements. Wheatley (1992) suggested that thinking beyond the future (which is linear), permeating organizational space, is the meeting of "field vision," where energy links with the field's vision to form or create behavior congruent with one's thoughts (pp. 53–54). *The Visionary Leader* (Wall et al., 1992) is based on the premise that a "vision" is one's projection of his perceptions, developed through awareness, having determined his core values and purpose. Wall contends that the strength of a leader's vision and his ability to articulate that vision to employees will be the measure of leadership in the Twenty-first Century.

The awareness, observation, witnessing or being mindful of one's mind or state-of-being (including the dialogue within oneself or with another), with or without verbal or written symbols of communication.[19]

PRACTICAL WORK APPLICATIONS

Each of us lives each day with the results of our voice: our choices, our associations, and our values. It is therefore imperative that we comprehend the responsibilities and obstacles we burden ourselves with when we do not know, or listen to our Voice. Each of us is directly responsible for the "reality" we create and the effect of our Voice on others. For, while each of our voices are unique, each of us are interconnected. In other words our Voice is both the "cause" and the "effect" of reality in each other and ourselves.

VOICE CREATES SELF-DESCRIPTION

Leaders never take followers into the future with their voice; they bring the future back to their followers and impart the energy of the vision through their Voice so that each follower experiences the proposed outcome. In other words the Transformational Leader manipulates through motivation, experiential learning, and recognition of the follower's core needs, values, and understanding of "truth." Each of us are use to believing something is true because we "experience" it. The transformational leader goes the next step by allowing each follower to know something is true because they have now envisioned it.

The transformational leader allows each follower to become a vested engineer of the incremental steps approaching the vision. Each successful accomplishment, a mosaic piece of the vision, removes the association of fear from the conceptualized future. Many of us have fear of the future we create because we either do not believe we can create our future or we fail to believe that anything we create has value. Once each of us comprehends that we are responsible for our future we will start knowing, not just believing, the value of our energy. Once we value our energy, we will then carefully attend to our core values supporting our Voice and the manifestations our Voice constructs. Once we realize we always get the answer to our question, we will begin to question with wonderment and purposeful intent. And, once we realize that we are the manifestation of our last intent we will begin to comprehend the divine in our core values.

VOICE CREATES WORK ENVIRONMENT

It is imperative to recognize that others may not embrace your transformation. Most likely, others will challenge your transformation with equal resistance;

to the degree they are annoyed, inconvenienced, or required to change in some way. And, people who love and support you may make these challenges. So, when it comes to bullies, determinedly difficult people, and predators; realize that your transformation will be seen as a personal and direct threat: no they will not be pleased. Transformational Leadership is not for the faint at heart. The transformational leader must be aware of and comprehend his core values and intent; and his Voice must be internally consistent or his energy will not manifest form. Yes, our Voice, when we achieve internal consistency manifests form: but our Voice does not exist in isolation. Our energy co-exists, co-mingles, and co-creates with all other energy which is why it is crucial to neutralize bullies, determinedly difficult people, and the predators who live and work amongst us. Transforming, and in some cases transcending the raucous energy of transactional, self-centered, low vibrational people is the purpose of this book.

NOTES

1. The research focused on identifying the common voices, if any, among sacred values, proactive management principles, and community consciousness. The author derived the term "Leadership Voices ™ to represent the common element identified when leadership principles presented in Christian tenets (as practiced within the United States) are compared to proactive management principles. While this project focused on Christian tenets as a spiritual source, it is acknowledged and appreciated that other religions and "spiritual scriptures/writings/oral histories" may also be compatible with proactive management principles. This study made two assumptions, first leaders recognize that their voice creates work standards, principles and environment; and second, leaders acknowledge a personal spiritual or religious affiliation.

A mailed survey instrument was determined to be the best data collection method. To develop the survey instrument in a non-biased method and to reach the State's diverse business community, focus groups were formed. Focus group members were selected from the State's prominent 500 companies and religious leaders from the State's Interdenominational Counsel of Churches. This processed produced the qualitative data used to produce the study's survey instrument. The study's survey instrument was sent to a separate and distinct group of Washington State business executives, elected and appointed officials and community sages. No individual participated as both a focus group member and survey respondent.

A 35-question survey mailed to 250 Washington State elected and appointed officials, business executive officers, and community sages. The survey asked: Do survey participants have religious or spiritual affiliations; and if so, will they sate them? Can, and will, survey participants specifically articulate their work related leadership values, and ethic of care? To what degree do leaders acknowledge their personal voice creates or sustains the work environment? What are proactive management principles? To what degree do leader's voices create standards and principles?

The findings of this study are as follows: Leaders recognize their voice creates work standards, principles and the environment. Leaders acknowledge a personal spiritual or religious affiliation. Respondents believed their personal values (voice) significantly influence their work ethics. Respondents realized their religious or spiritual values guided or supported them in establishing and defining work policies and process. Respondents acknowledged their spiritual or sacred writings provide guidance when making management decisions. Respondents acknowledged their religious or spiritual beliefs influenced their leadership or management style.

Respondents acknowledged their religious or spiritual belief influenced/defined their standard(s) for work productivity. A little less than half of the respondents acknowledged their core belief(s) influenced/defined their standards for work productivity. Respondents who had significant input and control over their budgets indicated that their basic budget philosophy was either "overall benefit" or "bottom line." Respondents frequently selected the following 3 core values; integrity, family, and God.

2. Bellah, Robert N. et al, Habits of the Heart: Individualism and Commitment in American Life. (Harper and Row: New Yorkm, 1985). Bellah, Robert N. et al., The Good Society. (Alfred A. Knopf: New York, 1991). Peck, M. Scott, The Different Drum: Community-Making and Peace, (Simon and Schuster: New York, 1987).

3. The act of receiving energy from one system and re-transmitting the energy to another system in a different form. Contemporary research is focusing on the process of self-reflective information transduction focused in the limbic-hypothalamic system. This research is exploring the relationship, if any, between an individual's awareness of self and the philosophy of the limbic system of the brain and the hypothalamus's secretions of hormones that influence the pituitary gland. C. G. Jung was one of the early psychologists who explored internodal information transduction (biofeedback) as a therapeutic method. This self-reflective process is the beginning of the transcendent function, the collaboration of conscious and unconscious. C. G. Jung stopped short of equating consciousness and the creation of form. However, cosmic consciousness, has also been described as an awareness of the cosmos, life, and the order of the universe.

4. Hall, Brian P. and Helen Thompson, Leadership Through Values, (Paulist Press: New York, 1980).

5. Aziz, Robert, C.G. Jung's Psychology of Religion and Synchronicity. (State University of New York Press, 1990). Bucke, Richard M. (1923). Cosmic Consciousness: A Study in the Evolution of the Human Mind. (Penguin Books: New York, 1990). Herbert, Nick, Elemental Mind: Human Consciousness and The New Physics. (Plume: New York, 1993). McTaggart, Lynne, The Field: The Quest for the Secret Force of the Universe. (HarperCollins: New York, 2002). Wolinsky, Stephen, and The Way of the Human: Volume I Developing Multi-Dimensional Awareness. The Quantum Psychology Notebooks (Special section: Trances people live revised). (Quantum Institute: Capitola, Cali., 1999a).

6. Herbert, Nick, Elemental Mind: Human Consciousness and The New Physics. (Plume: New York, 1993). Herbert, Nick, Quantum Reality: Beyond the New Physics an Excursion into Metaphysics and The Meaning of Reality. (Anchor Books, Doubleday:

New York, 1985). Wolinsky, Stephen, Quantum Consciousness: The Guide to Experiencing Quantum Psychology, (Bramble Books: Northfork, Conn., 1993).

7. Herbert, Nick. Elemental Mind: Human Consciousness and The New Physics. (Plume: New York, 1993). Herbert, Nick, Quantum Reality: Beyond the New Physics an Excursion into Metaphysics and The Meaning of Reality. (Anchor Books, Doubleday: New York, 1985). Greene, Brian, The Elegant Universe: Superstrings, Hidden Dimensions, And the Quest for the Ultimate Theory. (W.W. Norton: New York, 2003). McTaggart, Lynne, The Field: The Quest for the Secret Force of the Universe. (HarperCollins: New York, 2002).

8. Wolinsky, Stephen, Quantum Consciousness: The Guide to Experiencing Quantum Psychology. (Bramble Books: Northfork, Conn., 1993), 17.

9. Bennis, Warren G, On Becoming A Leader. (Addison-Wesley: Menlo Park, 1989). Bolman, Lee G. and Terrence E. Deal, Reframing Organizations: Artistry, Choice, and Leadership. (Jossey-Bass: San Francisco, 1991). Burns James M, Leadership. (Harper and Row: New York, 1978). Gardiner, John. J, Building leadership teams. In M.F. Green (Ed.) Leaders for A New Era: Strategies for Higher Education. (American Council on Education/ MacMillan Publishing: New York, 1988), 137–153. Hall, Brian P. and Helen Thompson, Leadership Through Values, (Paulist Press: New York, 1980). Peck, M. Scott, A World Waiting To Be Born: Civility Rediscovered. (Bantam Books: New York, 1993).

10. Irby, Linda, Leadership Voices™: Values, Proactive Management, and Consciousness. (UMI: 304 1369, 2002).

11. Irby, Leadership Voices™, Values, 16.

12. Covey, Steven R., Principled Centered Leadership: Give A Man A Fish and you Feed Him for A Day; Teach Him How To Fish and You Feed Him for A Lifetime. (Simon and Schuster: New York, 1992). Evans, Patricia, The Verbally Abusive Relationship: How to Recognize It and How To Respond. (Bob Adams, Inc.: Holbrook, Massachusetts, 1992). Evans, Patricia, Verbal Abuse Survivors Speak Out: On Relationship and Recovery. (Bob Adams, Inc. Holbrook, Mass, 1993). Greenleaf, Robert. K, Servant Leadership: A Journey into the Nature of Legitimate Power and Greatness. (Paulist Press: New York, 1982). James, Jennifer, Windows. Expanded edition. (Newmarket Press: New York, 1987). Peck, M. Scott, A World Waiting To Be Born: Civility Rediscovered. (Bantam Books: New York, 1993).

13. Fruehling, Rosemary. T. and Joan M. Lacombe, Communicating for Results. (EMC Paradigm: St Paul, Minn., 1966). McKay, Mathew., et al., How to Communicate: The Ultimate Guide to Improving Your Personal and Professional Relationships. (MJF Books: New York, 1983). Wolinsky, Stephen, Quantum Consciousness: The Guide to Experiencing Quantum Psychology. Bramble Books: (Northfork, Conn., 1993).Wolinsky, Stephen, The Way of The Human: Volume I Developing Multi-Dimensional Awareness. The Quantum Psychology Notebooks (Special section: Trances people live revised). (Quantum Institute: Capitola, Cali. 1999a). Wolinsky, Stephen, The Way of the Human: Volume II the False Core and The False Self. The Quantum Psychology Notebooks. (Quantum Institute: Capitola, California, 1999b). Irby, Linda, Leadership Voices™: Values, Proactive Management, and Consciousness. (UMI: 304 1369, 2002).

14. Wolinsky, Stephen, The Way of the Human: Volume I Developing Multi-Dimensional Awareness. The Quantum Psychology Notebooks (Special section: Trances people live revised). (Quantum Institute: Capitola, Cali., 1999a), 34.

15. English, Harace B, and Ava C. English, A Comprehensive Dictionary of Psychological And Psychoanalytical Terms. A Guide to Usage, for Readers and Writers in the Fields of Psychology, Psychoanalysis, Psychiatry, Education, Guidance, and Social Work. (David McKay Company, Inc.: New York, 1966).

16. Rodale, Jerome I., The Synonym Finder: Special Deluxe Edition. Rodale Press: Emmaus, Pa., 1978).

17. Irby, Linda, Leadership Voices™: Values, Proactive Management, and Consciousness. (UMI: 304 1369, 2002).

18. Irby, Leadership Voices™, Values.

19. Wolinsky, Stephen, Quantum Consciousness: The Guide to Experiencing Quantum Psychology. (Bramble Books: Northfork, Conn., 1993).

Chapter Two

Energy and Quantum Consciousness

> When two quantum entities, A and B, briefly interact (via conventional local forces) then move apart beyond the range of initial interaction, quantum theory does not describe them as separate objects, but continues to regard them as a single entity. If one takes seriously this feature, called quantum inseparability, then all objects that have once interacted are in some sense still connected.
>
> Nick Herbert

Quantum theory was devised in the late 1920's to deal with the atom. Quantum theory's development has surpassed its inventor's most remote expectations. Initially, considered merely a tool of measurement, it evolved from primarily a measurement "tool" to a reflection of the fundamental unity of "all." No entity is so exotic that it escapes quantum rules. Quantum theory does not describe entities; it represents them—one description fits all.[20]

DISCUSSION OF CONSCIOUSNESS

Consciousness is the second necessary environment of human society; the first is the natural entity itself.[21] Consciousness is a concept linking the body and psyche, instinct and image.[22] All consciousness is of an indirect nature and affects (interprets) what is perceived.[23]

There are three forms or grades of consciousness: the Simple Consciousness, the Self-consciousness, and the Cosmic Consciousness. Cosmic Consciousness is a higher form of consciousness, both subjective and objective, which is cognizant of the cosmos, life, and the order of the universe. Along with cosmic consciousness, an intellectual enlightenment or illumination occurs, extending to a state of moral exaltation, producing an indescribable feeling of elation, and joyousness, quickening moral senses. With awareness there is a sense of immortality, a consciousness of eternal life — not a conviction that one shall have this, but the realization that one already has it.[24]

Consciousness involves bringing imagery (with its attendant affect) to the threshold of decision and action.[25] The need to link implies a differentiation of one from another. The term "other" does not have a self-evident connotation. The word "other" originated from the word "allos," which is grounded in several ancient languages. In Greek there are two words for "other:" allos and heteros. Both of these words are found in Modern English: allotheism—the worship of strange gods, and heterogeneous—composed of diverse elements. The word "allos" is also related to the Latin alter, and alienus, the root of alienation—otherness or estrangement. Finally, "allos" belongs to the same family as the Sanskrit ant-aras or our English word "other," meaning "many of" with a sense of difference. The word heteros not only has its Greek roots but also relates to the Sanskrit eka-tara which means one-of-two, which has the following meanings: on one side, harmony, conjunction, solidarity, same, unanimity. Finally, the Sanskrit root "eka" can be traced to the Latin "aequus" or our English "equal."

The consequence of the linguistic family roots of the word "other" indicates that this word inherently contains the contradictory definitions of difference, separation, sameness, interior, main substance, and harmony. Therefore, in the context of discussions about the "self" and the "selves" need to differentiate from the "other," the correct implication is that the differentiation is from the rest of the soul. This translation implies that there is still some "other" part of the psyche that constitutes the "rest" of the "self" of which we are conscious. Therefore, the inherent dual meaning of the word "other" may best be comprehended as: if the "rest" is added to the existing part a wholeness, a totality may be achieved; but if the "rest" is left apart, then a separation, a division results.[26] This linguistic trail identifies the singular voice of Consciousness and Community. (It is important to remember that Jung (1991) never presented an explicit or systematic theory of the "other" as such, although his implication of the "other's" meaning is implicit throughout his entire works.)

There is an increasing concurrence, from various disciplines, that the "self" as an awareness continuously "struggles" with the paradox of the need for both individuality and inclusiveness from and with the "other." This "struggle" of the "self" for wholeness from the "other" is explained as follows:

1. From a unified field, individual notions of "self" arise. First, something appears for which there is no know antecedent. The ensuing universal, age-old questions of: (a) where does the "self" that is organizing originate? (b) Why does it attempt to separate itself from the unified field? (c) Why

does this movement toward differentiation even start? These questions, as well as many others, are currently unanswered. Sages and scientist both simply state that this is where the world as we know it originates.[27]

Everything that follows from this act of "appearance" seeks differentiation. This process of "self" and differentiation is paradoxical. To exist, the "self" must create a boundary. Yet "self" cannot survive behind the boundary it creates. If the "self" does not remember its connnectedness, then the "self" ceases to exist.[28]

2. Life co-evolves; there are no separate individuals.[29]
3. The co-evolutionary process of life cannot support isolation; even our boundaries create an environment for others. We separate ourselves, but we also create the conditions for one another's life. One self-asserting being creates itself, and its presence creates conditions for others to take form.[30]

Consciousness manifests itself at various levels: the two primary forms are practical and discursive. Consciousness, or awareness, can be ascribed to both individuals and collective entities or groups.[31] Consciousness may also be considered as a super-individual relational network that binds ideas, beliefs, concepts, and comprehensive blocks of ideology, doctrines, creeds, theories, and traditions.[32]

DISCUSSION OF QUANTUM CONSCIOUSNESS

Quantum theory, devised in the late 1920's to explain or account for the properties of the atom, has surpassed its theorists' most remote expectations. Initially considered merely a tool to be primarily used to assist in measurement, it evolved into a significant and primal paradigm reflecting the fundamental unity of "all," No entity is so exotic that it escapes quantum rules. Quantum theory does not describe entities; it represents them—one description fits all.[33]

Quantum measurement contends that energy creates form. Different approaches to quantum measurement, of which the prevailing ones are Copenhagen's, Von Neumann's, and the Neorealist model, each has it drawback and none gives a completely satisfactory picture of the measurement act.[34] Wolinsky, whose 12-year study of self-observation culminated in *Quantum Consciousness* (1993), asserts that in the act of self-observation, "the witness not only witnesses and is mindful of what passes through the mind and body, but is also the creative source of it."[35] Wolinsky concurs with Heinsburg's Uncertainty Principle that our mental state consists of basic forms of energy and that our reality is observer created. Self-observation (the observer) and that which is created (thoughts, feelings, sensations, beliefs, etc.) are fundamentally identical.

Wolinsky's assertion is consistent with David Bohm's idea that there are an "explicit order" and an "implicit order." The explicit order is the world as we typically perceive it; the implicate order is the unbroken wholeness that connects us all. At the quantum level, objects, particles, people, and emotions are made, subatomically, of the same substance. At the quantum (subatomic) level, the composition of what we experience as space and what we experience as physical matter is identical. There is no difference between space (emptiness) and physical matter. In Einstein's words, "Everything is emptiness and form is condensed emptiness."[36]

Dr. Heisenberg's Uncertainty Principle demonstrated that the observer creates that which she observes. The implication is that thought and the observer-of-thought are not two separate phenomena.[37]

Simply put, Quantum energy contends that energy creates form. Heinsburg's Uncertainty Principle contends that our mental state consists of basic forms of energy. The deduction then is that your Voice (your intent—either external or internal) creates form. Voice is energy, energy creates form.

DISCUSSION OF COMMUNITY CONSCIOUSNESS

Social consciousness or community consciousness must be treated as one of the distinguishing attributes of social systems. Social systems are peculiar in that their entities, processes, and relationships emerge from, and are constituted by, the actions of their members and these actions, in turn, are predicted in the voice of community members. In other words, social systems are "image directed." That is, social systems are entities for which the knowledge of "itself" (the system) is a significant part of its own dynamics, which in turn changes the system.[38]

Consciousness, whether individual, collective or social, emanates from a single source, "a pool of resources, concepts, symbols, codes, and frames" for interpretations. One's level of consciousness either keeps one blind to possible constraints or opportunities, or allows one's eyes to open to all possibilities. One's level of consciousness either supplies inadequate tools for grasping reality or allows one the possibility of debunking illusions by offering sharp, critical notions: either of these possibilities is a natural condition.[39]

Community consciousness, a gargantuan force, is a living regenerative "pool" from which individuals construct their paradigms.

All living systems have the ability to self-produce. Because a living system produces itself, deciding what it will be and how it will operate, it enjoys enormous freedom. It is free to create itself as it desires. At the beginning, this creative expression is not bounded by any external constraints. Life makes itself up by exercising its freedom, by experimenting with different forms, by asserting different meanings. The freedom to discern and to choose lies at the heart of life. We are free to notice what we will. . . . We each create our own worlds by what we choose to notice; [sic] creating a world of distinctions that makes sense to us. We then "see" the world through this self we have created. Information from the external world is a minor influence. We connect who we are with selected amounts of new information to enact our particular version of reality. . . Because information from the outside plays such a small role in our perceptions. . . . We can never direct a living system. We can only disturb it. As external agents, we provide only small impulses of information. We can nudge, titillate, or provoke one another into some new ways of seeing. However, we can never give anyone an instruction and expect him or her to follow it precisely. We can never assume that anyone else sees the world as we do.[40]

In wide concurrence, interdisciplinary scholars and leaders assert that community consciousness:

1. Is a collective reservoir of psychic possibilities.[41]
2. Is aroused by awareness or recognition.[42]
3. Is often considered to be one's intuition.[43]
4. Requires one to "appreciation" her awareness or growth is not possible.[44]
5. The manifestation of form from energy (accomplishing one's goals) requires both reflection and internal congruence.[45]
6. Manifesting form from energy requires the discernment and synthesis (of concepts and ideas) to manifest representative "forms" symbolizing the collective good or concerns.[46]
7. Individuals can develop their awareness of community consciousness through training, which is most effective when it is experiential (with repetition for practice) and is enhanced when immediately followed by didactic instruction.[47]

The outcome of one's awareness of community consciousness is a healthy, competent, effective, and congruent community.[48] Hitt (1990) enumerates the principal features of community consciousness to be:

1. A valid energy of "belief."
2. A reality or experience common to all.
3. A "point" conceived and shared by all.
4. A "clarity" which is inherently congruent.

5. A "clarity" conceived identically by all.
6. A coercive certainty that "is" knowledge.
7. A recognition of universal interrelatedness.

A community is more than the sum of its parts; it is a living organism in its own right. Leaders should focus on the community as a whole, not on individual needs and characteristics of the community. Failure to focus on the community as a whole impedes development of the community. Generally, leaders should restrict their interventions to interpretations of community behavior, instead of addressing the behavior of individuals.[49] Here is another paradox. To exist, the self must create a boundary. Yet no self can survive behind the boundary it creates. If it does not remember its connectedness, the self will expire.[50]

Simply put, your place of work is your work community. Your work community, a living entity, is greater than the some of its individual members. Those in administrative authority must comprehend, nurture, and serve the needs of the entire workplace, not isolated individuals. If the behavior of the work community, as an entirety is considered, paradoxically, the rights of individuals must be recognized for the benefit of the connected whole. Bullies, determinedly difficult people, and predators do not recognize boundaries; therefore the survival of the work community is perilous. Voice is energy, energy creates form.

DISCUSSION OF COMMUNITY

Some individuals may believe they can exist and succeed in isolation. However, when an individual fails to contribute to others, he becomes irrelevant. If his self-expression is not meaningful to others, the individual will go unnoticed or be rejected.[51] Seemingly paradoxically, when he opens himself to others, he not only forms the link to others, but he also opens himself to greater creative expression. On the other hand, when he retains autonomy, he develops his own personal sense of collective "aloneness." It is in this state of "aloneness" that each of us discovers new meaning and is able to transform.[52] Therefore, in this continuous cycle of personal autonomy and inclusiveness, each person struggles with "self" and "others," as collectively we build communities that are reflections of this struggle.

Community neither comes naturally nor is purchased cheaply.[53] There is joy, a feeling of freedom, and a healing power in genuine Community[54] Community is more than the sum of its parts, the individual members. The most salient characteristics of a true community are: inclusivity, commitment, consciousness, realism, contemplation, and spirit. Community must be a safe place for all individuals, a laboratory for personal disarmament so that when necessary, individuals can "fight gracefully." A community must provide an opportunity for each person to personally contribute and be acknowledged.[55] Finally, a community is a group of leaders, not a group led by individuals or cliques.[56]

Community, within the context of spirit, takes pride in the "collective." Individuals within a community take pride in achieving through collective efforts, realizing that achievement through collective collaboration creates something greater than the "whole." There is nothing competitive about the spirit of the community; the spirit is one of peace.[57] The sprit of community is not limited only to "Christian tenets." For those who have a Christian orientation, community is the beginning of preparing for the Holy ascent: community is the manifestation of the Holy Spirit.[58]

Virtually any group of people can accomplish building community if the members know what they are doing. The vast majority of people are capable of learning the rules of community.[59] Forming a community by design entails:

- a lawful process;
- principles of good communication, which are principles of good community (both words are from the same root);
- awareness of how community is achieved and practiced;
- purposeful construction of community rather than a "stumbling" into community by chance or unconsciousness;
- simple teaching and conscious learning of the rules of both communication and community, allowing practice of the rules; and
- experiential learning (more demanding but also more effective than passive learning) of the rules of communication and community.

Some of the properties necessary to build a community (chaos, emptiness, expectations and preconceptions, ideology/theology, solutions, and issues of control) may also be barriers to building the community.[60] The transformation of a collection of individuals into a group, and then into a community of individuals, requires each community member to relinquish some personal prerogative.[61] The dynamics of the making of a community, either in its development or its maintenance, includes:

1. Flight: a group shows a strong inclination or tendency to flee from issues and problems.
2. Fight: this aspect of community tends to predominate during the second stage of community building. Sometimes this stage of development is

called chaos. It is necessary for a leader to "guide" the group through this phase to a solution.

3. Pairing: the forming of alliances of several individuals, consciously or unconsciously, on issues that lose sight of building a community. This process interferes with the group's maturation.

4. Dependency: a devastating and difficult dysfunction for communities to combat.[62]

Once a community has been built, it must be maintained. Parameters that most frequently are the subjects of tension include size, structure, authority, inclusively, intensity, commitment, individuality, task definition, and rituals.[63] There is a point beyond which our self-determination not only becomes inaccurate and prideful, but increasingly self-defeating. The reality is that we are inevitably social creatures; we desperately need each other, not merely for sustenance or only for company but also for meaning in our lives. From this paradox come the seeds that grow community.[64]

Bellah et al. (1985[65]) reports that most people interviewed were serious, engaged, deeply involved in the world. However, insofar as people are limited to a language of radical individual autonomy, many do not think of themselves, or others, except as arbitrary centers of "will." A way out of this dead-ended radical individualism– inherited from Wordsworth, Emerson, and other romantics—is to assume that the core of every person is in fundamental spiritual harmony that links her not only to every other person but to the cosmos as a whole.

Such an assumption does not affront our concept of the "self." External authority, cultural tradition, and social institutions all can be eschewed. Rather than negating or diminishing the "self," the "self" in all its pristine purity is affirmed. Somehow that "self," once discovered, turns out to be at one with the universe.

Referring to Bellah's works on individualism, Peck (1987[66]) states that our individualism must be counterbalanced by commitment. As one's individualism breaks down, the transformation begins.[67] Samuels et al. (1993[68]) discusses Jung's contention that the paradox is between an individual becoming him or her "self"—whole, indivisible, and distinct from other people—and the individual's need to adapt to the "collective's" norms, standards, precepts, mores, and values. Peck (1987) emphasizes that the relationship between individualism and commitment to building and sustaining community must be contemplated by both the individuals in the community, and the "community" as an entity.[69]

A safe community is achieved through awareness. Peck contends that there is no such thing as an instant community under ordinary circumstances. It takes a great deal of work for a group of strangers to strive toward and achieve the safety of a true community. However, once an individual feels safe enough to share his personal vulnerability—and is allowed to share another's vulnerability—the "flood gates" of communication open.[70] Within the community offering a safe place to experiment, one is offered the opportunity to open to communication.

Realism within the context of community is necessary. The existence of realism within community supports individuals who think and "buck" the trends.[71] Such individualism within community and distinctions made in favor of the individual prevent "group think" or "mob psychology."

However, "community" is also a group that can fight gracefully. To become such requires commitment. Cliques, factions, and "sides" must be given up. The members must know how to listen to each other and how to reject each other's proposals, usually through achieving consensus.[72]

On the other hand, a "community," within the context of being a group of all leaders, is a group that has achieved decentralized authority. The community is antitotalitarian; consensus determines the "final" decision.[73]

Scarcity moves us to explore more diversified ways of interacting so that we can continue to live together.[74] This is the process of specialization. In the past, we have looked at "competition" as an explanation of our behaviors. However, Wheatley and Kellner-Rodgers believe that scarcity leads only to increased fights for survival, and increased specialization of individuals, not to competition between and among individuals.

Simply put, through association there is assimilation. If you work around bullies, determinedly difficult people, and predators you will either take on their characteristics or sooner or later be forced out. You can not give what you do not have. So, if your work community continuously models self-centeredness, abusiveness, and domination your interpersonal relationships and customer service will copy these characteristics. Voice is energy, energy creates form.

AWARENESS PRECEDES APPEARANCE

Quantum consciousness is Wolinsky's (1993) name for the application of quantum psychology to problem resolution. Quantum consciousness asks the individual to practice the philosophy that "Everything is made of emptiness and form is condensed emptiness."[75] Quantum consciousness is essentially a unity consciousness—the awareness that an underlying "unity" connects us all.[76]

The quantum approach provides a way to recognize unity consciousness that is both experiential and practical, enabling people to develop a new context in which problem resolution can occur more easily.[77] The quantum ap-

proach arises from a perception of the relativity of beliefs; it asks one to recognize the validity of the paradigm from one's subjective experience only.
Quantum consciousness is not about integrating anything; it is about recognizing and experiencing the underlying unity, the underlying absence or in-
terconnection of all parts. This underlying experience of unity is where the
true wholeness can be experienced and actually is the context for everything;
it is the context that already is. Quantum consciousness as discussed entails
seven different levels:

1. Level 1. "As the observer of the contents of one's mind (thoughts, feeling,
   emotions, sensations, associations), comprehension includes self is more
   than the mind's contents."[78]
2. Level 2. "Everything (thoughts, feelings, emotions, sensations, associations) is made of energy. Once the leader has experienced his "self," then
   he can begin to experience how all that is observed is made of the same
   underlying energy. At this level the leader, or manager, "masters" her ability to dispense with "labels." As mastery at this level seasons, one's comprehension and discernment increases, and the leader or manager comprehends that awareness precedes appearance.[79]
3. Level 3. There is no reality in the absence of observation, and that observation creates reality,[80] demonstrated by Heisenberg as the "Uncertainty
   Principle." The importance of this level to leaders and managers is that
   they are empowered to take the "quantum leap," moving beyond the passive witness to the active involvement of creating. Here the importance of
   the self-fulfilling prophecy phenomena is amplified. Self-fulfilling
   prophecies not only reassure or distress our personal conception or reality,
   they are reality creating.[81]
4. Level 4. The physical universe is made of time.[82] By cogitation, reflection,
   and experience leaders and managers "unfold" time as a concept created
   by humans. The "art" of timing, patience, tolerance, and stamina for one's
   "self" and others is developed in Level 5.
5. Level 5. The physical universe is made of energy, space, mass, and time.[83]
   The leader or manager is now equipped, for the first time, to acknowledge
   and appreciate the changeless nature of space and to explore how our
   awareness is transformed by this recognition. The deliberate recognition
   of energy, space, mass and time creates a textural comprehension of the
   underlying unity of all. We as creators are the recipients or objects of our
   creation, and everything and everyone is made of the same substance (at
   the subatomic level).
6. Level 6. Everything interpenetrates everything else.[84] Physicist David
   Bohm of London's Birkbeck College has especially stressed the necessary

wholeness of the quantum world. Quantum wholeness is a fundamentally new kind of togetherness, undiminished by spatial and temporal separation. No casual hook-up, this wholeness is, rather, a true mingling of distant being that reaches across the galaxy as forcefully as it reaches across the garden.[85]

Bohm's discovery that the universe is an "unfolding" and "enfolding" of four main elements (energy, space, mass, and time (duration)) more fully explains the implications of energy described in Level 2. All boundaries are observer-created rather than inherent. This is the quantum jump that takes consciousness beyond "simply" judgments and evaluations and introduces us to the experience of underlying unity.

7. Level 7. Everything is made of the same substance.[86] "Everything is made of emptiness, and form is condensed emptiness" a statement that has been attributed to Einstein. Everything in the physical universe has form; form creates what Bohm called the explicit order of sizes, shapes, mass, and density. In order for there to be separate forms, there have to be consensual boundaries that create the appearance of a distinction between you and me. The consensual boundaries constitute how we normally perceive the world. When we comprehend that what we perceive as dense and physical objects are composed of the same particles and waves, then the limited, isolating experience of you-ness and me-ness dissolves.[87]

One is led to a new notion of unbroken wholeness, which denies the classical ability of dividing the world into two separately and independently existing parts. The inseparable quantum interconnectedness of the whole universe is the fundamental reality."

Stephen Wolinsky

Quantum theory, in a certain sense, regards the world as made out of waves (like waves in one's bathtub) rather than out of things. Quantum entities and their attributes combine according to the rules of wave addition rather than according to the rules of ordinary arithmetic. When waves meet, their amplitudes add, as stated in the rule called the "superposition principal." The superposition principle is as important in the quantum world as arithmetic is for everyday life. Quantum waves are oscillations of possibility; they carry no energy at all; for this reason sometimes they are called "empty waves." Whenever waves of the same frequency (spatial or temporal) come together with identical phases, they are said to be "in phase;" waves whose phases differ by half a cycle are "out of phase." A quantum wave's intensity (amplitude squared) is a measure of probability. Because the quantum wave carries no energy, it is not directly detectable — we never see any quantum waves, only quantum particles.

Quantum theory predicts the results of measurement with unsurpassed accuracy, so physicists use quantum theory to measure the world itself, because former "particles" now show their wave aspects, and former "waves" behave like particles. Quantum theory reflects the fundamental unity of being, by describing all "quons" the same way: "One description fits all."[88] However, the term "describes" is a bit misleading because quantum theory does not "describe" entities at all, it represents them. Quantum theory applies to all physical entities without exception.

Numerous authors' discussions of leadership and management actually are describing the experience of the "end point" of quantum consciousness, the "fundamental freedom." At this point the separated, individual self-hood is transcended to arrive at community consciousness.[89]

VOICE IS ENERGY, ENERGY CREATES FORM

How we choose to label an emotion or thought influences our internal, subjective experience. A former decision about an experience, a former belief about the world, prevents us from allowing in new information. Hence, through our label, we experience and condense an emotion into a part- (icle), which is condensed energy. Due to the fixed nature of our thoughts or beliefs, the condensed energy, which has become a part- (icle), begins to become more dense energy or mass—energy creates form.

Stephen Wolinsky

Wolinsky's quantum consciousness theory is the leading hypothesis regarding the creation of form from energy. Wolinsky's formulation draws on theories of quantum reality, developed regarding quantum measurement. In the classical Copenhagen interpretation, both the quantum system and a measuring device are envisioned as theoretically inaccessible. The wave function is seen as a mere technical tool that expresses the relationship existing between two radically different kinds of being. In John Von Neumann's all-quantum interpretation, both the system and the measuring device are represented as proxy waves. To make this description work, the system's waveform must "collapse" during a measurement. In Neorealist interpretations, everything, both system and measuring device, are envisioned as being made of particles that interact with one another via invisible supraliminal waves.

None of these three approaches to quantum measurement gives a completely satisfactory picture of the measurement act—the "miracle"—the creation of form. The Copenhagen interpretation endows the measuring instrument with magical properties (for instance, the ability to reduce possibility to actuality) while removing the instrument in principle from logical analysis.

Von Neumann's interpretation restores the measuring instrument to an equal status with the rest of the world, but transfers its magical properties to a mysterious and elusive event (the collapse). The Neorealist's interpretation sanctifies neither measuring device or measurement act. Neorealist measurements are ordinary interactions, but the existence of an invisible supraliminal force field must be assumed.

Von Neumann called the collapse of the wave the "quantum jump." The creation of form, according to Von Neumann, is the location of the division between the system and the measuring device. Von Neumann demonstrated that one could cut the wave and insert a "collapse" anywhere one pleased. This meant that cutting the wave offers no clues concerning where to locate the division between system and the measuring device. Finally, Von Neumann concluded that the human consciousness is the site of the wave function collapse; energy creates form.[90]

Many physicists have rejected the unsatisfactory state of the Copenhagen, Von Neumann, and Neorealist models. Solutions "less drastic" than those discussed are being attempted. A distinctive quantum approach to explaining the creation of form from energy is advanced by Erwin Stronger. Schrodinger regarded experiments to determine whether phase randomization collapses the wave function. Schrodinger determined that although phase randomization may certainly scramble a "quon's" path, it is unlikely that the "quon" is destroyed. The law of the realm guarantees that a quon's possibilities can never be reduced below an action quantum.[91] The "bottom line" to Schrodinger's experiment is that eventually one has to admit: "And the miracle occurs;" energy creates form.

Simply put, quantum physicists agree that energy creates form. Their experiments have shown the occurrence, but precisely where in the "wave" and exactly how form is created has remained elusive. Quantum physicists also concur that the quantum leap from energy to form is the occurrence of the "miracle."

Your "Voice" creates form. Do you know your core values? Particularly if you are the administrative leader of your organization or work unit, the values of those to whom you delegate administrative authority are agents for you. You are getting what you "asked for," from those you lead and supervise? Do you like going to work? Do you want what you have manifested?

NOTES

20. Herbert, Nick, *Quantum Reality: Beyond the New Physics an Excursion into Metaphysics and The Meaning of Reality*. (Anchor Books, Doubleday: New York, 1985), 94–98.

21. Sztompka, Piotr, *The Sociology of Social Change*. (Blackwell, Oxford U.K. and Cambridge U.S.A.1993), 2–20.

22. Samuels, Aandrew, et al., *A Critical Dictionary of Jungian Analysis*. (Routledge and Kegan Paul LTD: New York, 1993), 26.

23. Samuels et al., A Critical, 117.

24. Bucke, Richard M., *Cosmic Consciousness: A Study in the Evolution of the Human Mind*. (Penguin Books: New York, 1990).

25. Samuels, A *Critical*, 128.

26. Jung, Carl. G., *The Undiscovered Self: With Symbols and the Interpretation of Dreams*. In the Revised Translation by R. F. C. Hull with a new introduction by W. McGuire. From Volume 10 of the Collected Works of C. G. Jung, *Civilization in Transition* (Second Edition). (Bollingen Series: Princeton University Press, 1990), 55–56

27. Alder, Ronald B. and Neil Towne, *Looking Out/Looking In* (7th ed.). (Harcourt Brace Jovanovich College Publishers: Fla., 1993). Aziz, Robert, *C.G. Jung's Psychology of Religion and Synchronicity*. (State University of New York Press, 1990). Bucke, Richard M. (1923). *Cosmic Consciousness: A Study in The Evolution of The Human Mind*. (Penguin Books: New York, 1990). Chopra, Deepak, *The Higher Self*. (Simon and Schuster: New York, 1993). Chopra, Deepak, *The Seven Spiritual Laws of Success: A Practical Guide to the Fulfillment of Your Dreams*. (Amber-Allen Publishing: San Rafael, Cal., 1994). Davison, Gerald D. and John M. Neil, *Abnormal Psychology: Fifth Edition*. (John Wiley and Sons: New York, 1990). Gleick, James, *Chaos: Making A New Science*. (Penguin Books: New York, 1987). Jung, Carl. G. (1969). *The Psychological Foundations of Belief in Spirits and The Soul and Death*. Extracted from Volume 8, *The Structure and Dynamics of the Psyche* (2nd ed.). (Princeton University Press, 1969). Jung, Carl. G. (1969). *The Psychological Foundations of Belief in Spirits and The Soul and Death*. Extracted from Volume 8, *The Structure and Dynamics of the Psyche* (2nd ed.). (Princeton University Press, 1969). Jung, Carl. G., *Psychology and the Occult*. Translation by R. F. C. Hull. From the Collected Works of C. G. Jung, Volumes 1, 8, and 18. (Bollingen Series: Princeton University Press.,1977). Jung, Carl. G., *The Undiscovered Self: With Symbols and the Interpretation of Dreams*. In the Revised Translation by R. F. C. Hull with a new introduction by W. McGuire. From Volume 10 of the Collected Works of C. G. Jung, *Civilization in Transition* (Second Edition). (Bollingen Series: Princeton University Press, 1990). Greene, Brian, *The Elegant Universe: Superstrings, Hidden Dimensions, And the Quest for The Ultimate Theory*. (W.W. Norton: New York, 2003). McTaggart, Lynne, *The Field: The Quest for the Secret Force of the Universe*. (HarperCollins: New York, 2002). 1991). Papadopoulos, Renos K. And Graham S. Saayman. (Eds.)., *Jung In Modern Perspective: The Master And His Legacy*. (Unity Press: Australia, 1991). Wheatley, Margaret J, *Leadership and The New Science: Learning About Organization from an Orderly Universe*. (Berrett-Koehler: San Francisco, 1992). Wheatley, Margaret. J. and Myron Kellner-Rogers, *A Simpler Way*. (Berrett-Koehler: San Francisco, 1996). Wolinsky, Stephen, *The Way Of The Human: Volume II The False Core And The False Self. The Quantum Psychology Notebooks*. (Quantum Institute: Capitola, California, 1999b).

28. Alder & Towne, 1993; Jung, 1990, 1991; Wheatley, 1992; Wheatley & Kellner-Rogers, 1996.

29. Bellah, 1985, 1991; Eisler, 1987; Gwaltney, 1981; Johansen & Swigart, 1994; Peck, 1987; Rubin, 1976; Terkel, 1986, 1995; *The New York Times*, 1996; Wheatley, 1992, 1996; Wiley, 1991.

30. Wheatley, Margaret. J. and Myron Kellner-Rogers, *A Simpler Way*. (Berrett-Koehler: San Francisco, 1996), 51.

31. Sztompka, *The Sociology*, 221.

32. Sztompka, Piotr, *The Sociology*, 222.

33. Herbert, Nick, *Quantum Reality*, 94–98.

34. Herbert, *Quantum Reality*, 148.

35. Wolinsky, Stephen, *Quantum Consciousness: The Guide to Experiencing Quantum Psychology*. (Bramble Books: Northfork, Conn., 1993), 12.

36. Wolinsky, *Quantum Consciousness*, 7.

37. Wolinsky, Quantum Consciousness, 17.

38. Sztompka, Piotr, *The Sociology of Social Change*. (Blackwell, Oxford U.K. and Cambridge U.S.A., 1993), 222.

39. Sztompka, The*e Sociology*, 222–223.

40. Wheatley, Margaret. J. and Myron Kellner-Rogers, *A Simpler Way*. (Berrett-Koehler: San Francisco, 1996), 47–49.

41. Gleick, James, Chaos: Making A New Science. (Penguin Books: New York, 1987). Jung, Carl. G. (1969). The Psychological Foundations of Belief in Spirits and The Soul and Death. Extracted from Volume 8, The Structure and Dynamics of the Psyche (2nd ed.). (Princeton University Press, 1969). Jung, Carl. G., Psychology and the Occult. Translation by R. F. C. Hull. From the Collected Works of C. G. Jung, Volumes 1, 8, and 18. (Bollingen Series: Princeton University Press.,1977). Jung, Carl. G., The Undiscovered Self: With Symbols and the Interpretation of Dreams. In the Revised Translation by R. F. C. Hull with a new introduction by W. McGuire. From Volume 10 of the Collected Works of C. G. Jung, Civilization in Transition (Second Edition). (Bollingen Series: Princeton University Press, 1990). Papadopoulos, Renos K. And Graham S. Saayman. (Eds.)., *Jung In Modern Perspective: The Master And His Legacy. (*Unity Press: Australia, 1991). Samuels, Aandrew, et al., A *Critical Dictionary of Jungian Analysis*. (Routledge and Kegan Paul LTD: New York, 1993). Wheatley, Margaret J, *Leadership and The New Science: Learning About Organization from an Orderly Universe*. (Berrett-Koehler: San Francisco, 1992). Wolinsky, Stephen, *Quantum Consciousness: The Guide to Experiencing Quantum Psychology*. (Bramble Books: Northfork, Conn., 1993).

42. Bucke, Richard M. (1923). *Cosmic Consciousness: A Study in The Evolution of The Human Mind. (*Penguin Books: New York, 1990). Edelman, Joel and M. B. Crain, *The Tao Of Negotiation: How You Can Prevent, Resolve And Transcend Conflict In Work And Everyday Life. (*Harper Business: New York,1993). Gardiner, John. J., *Beyond Leader and Community: Creating New Metaphors Of Governance For American Higher Education*. Article. (Seattle, Wash., 1993). Gilbreath, Robert D, *Escape From Management Hell: 12 Tales of Horror, Humor, And Heroism*. (Berrett-Koehler Publishers: San Francisco, 1993). Gretz, Karl. F. and Steven R. Drozdeck, *Empowering Innovative People. (*Prous Publishing Company: Chicago, 1992). Gwaltney, John L., *Drylongso: A Self-Portrait of Black America*. Vintage Books: New York. 1996). Naisbitt,

John. And Patricia Aburdene, *Megatrends 2000: Ten New Directions for the 1990's.* (William Morrow And Co., Inc.: New York, 1990). Oakley, Ed and Doug Krug, *Enlightened Leadership: Getting to the Heart Of Change.* Fireside: New York, 1991). Peck, M. Scott, *The Different Drum: Community-Making and Peace.* Simon and Schuster: (New York, 1987). Popcorn, Faith, *The Popcorn Report: Faith Popcorn on the Future of Your Company, Your World, Your Life.* Doubleday Currency: New York, 1991). Terry, Robert. W., *Authentic Leadership: Courage in Action.* (Jossey-Bass: San Francisco,1993). Wiley, Ralph., *Why Black People Tend to Shout: Cold Facts and Wry Views From a Black Man's World.* (Penguin Books: New York, 1991*)*.

43. Eisler, Riane., *The Chalice and The Blade: Our History, Our Future.* (Harper: San Francisco, 1987). Forbes, Beverly A. (1991). *Profile Of The Leader Of The Future: Origin, Premises, Values And Characteristics Of The Theory F Transformational Leadership Model.* Unpublished manuscript. Seattle, Wash., October 1993. Jung, Carl. G., *The Undiscovered Self: With Symbols and the Interpretation of Dreams.* In the Revised Translation by R. F. C. Hull with a new introduction by W. McGuire. From Volume 10 of the Collected Works of C. G. Jung, *Civilization in Transition* (Second Edition). (Bollingen Series: Princeton University Press, 1990). Kouzes, James. M. and Barry Z. Posner., *Credibility: How Leaders Gain And Lose It, Why People Demand It.* (Jossey-Bass: San Francisco, 1993).

44. Eisler, Riane., *The Chalice and The Blade: Our History, Our Future.* (Harper: San Francisco, 1987). Forbes, Beverly A. (1991). *Profile Of The Leader Of The Future: Origin, Premises, Values And Characteristics Of The Theory F Transformational Leadership Model.* Unpublished manuscript. Seattle, Wash., October 1993. Jung, Carl. G., *The Undiscovered Self: With Symbols and the Interpretation of Dreams.* In the Revised Translation by R. F. C. Hull with a new introduction by W. McGuire. From Volume 10 of the Collected Works of C. G. Jung, *Civilization in Transition* (Second Edition). (Bollingen Series: Princeton University Press, 1990).

45. Bucke, Richard M. (1923). Cosmic Consciousness: A Study in The Evolution of The Human Mind. (Penguin Books: New York, 1990). Chopra, Deepak, The Higher Self. (Simon and Schuster: New York, 1993). Chopra, Deepak, The Seven Spiritual Laws of Success: A Practical Guide to the Fulfillment of Your Dreams. (Amber-Allen Publishing: San Rafael, Cal., 1994). Covey, Steven R., *Principled Centered Leadership: Give A Man A Fish and You Feed Him For A Day; Teach Him How To Fish And You Feed Him For A Lifetime.* (Simon and Schuster: New York, 1992). DePree, Max, *Leadership Jazz.* (Doubleday: New York, 1992). Eisler, Riane., *The Chalice and The Blade: Our History, Our Future.* (Harper: San Francisco, 1987). Greene, Brian, *The Elegant Universe: Superstrings, Hidden Dimensions, And the Quest for The Ultimate Theory.* (W.W. Norton: New York, 2003). Herbert, Nick, *Quantum Reality: Beyond the New Physics an Excursion into Metaphysics and The Meaning of Reality.* (Anchor Books, Doubleday: New York, 1985). Herbert, Nick. *Elemental Mind: Human Consciousness and The New Physics.* (Plume: New York, 1993). Jung, Carl. G. (1969). *The Psychological Foundations of Belief in Spirits and The Soul and Death.* Extracted from Volume 8, *The Structure and Dynamics of the Psyche* (2nd ed.). (Princeton University Press, 1969). McTaggart, Lynne, *The Field: The Quest for the Secret Force of the Universe.* (HarperCollins: New York, 2002). Watzlawick, Paul,

The Invented Reality: How Do We Know What We Believe We Know? (Contributions To Constructivism). (W.W. Norton and Company, 1984).

46. Evans, Patricia, The Verbally Abusive Relationship: How to Recognize It and How To Respond. (Bob Adams, Inc.: Holbrook, Massachusetts, 1992). Evans, Patricia, Verbal Abuse Survivors Speak Out: On Relationship and Recovery. (Bob Adams, Inc. Holbrook, Mass.,1993). Farson, Richard, Management of the Absurd: Paradoxes in Leadership. (Simon and Schuster: New York, 1996). 1982). Keirsey, David and Marilyn Bates, Please Understand Me: Character and Temperament Types. (Prometheus Nemesis: Del Mar, Cal., 1984). 1973). Rubin, Harriet, *The Princessa: Machiavelli for Women*. (Currency: New York, 1997). Rubin, Lillian B, *Worlds of Pain: Life in the Working-Class Family*. (Basic Books, Inc., Publishers: New York, 1976). Simons, George F., et al., *Transcultural Leadership: Empowering the Diverse Workforce*. Gulf Publishing Company: Houston, 1993). Terkel, Studs, *Hard Times: An Oral History of the Great Depression*. (Pantheon Books: New York, 1986). Terkel, Studs, Coming of Age: The Story of Our Century By Those Who've Lived It. (The New Press: New York, 1995). West, Cornel, *Race Matters*. (Beacon Press: Boston, 1991).

47. Peck, M. Scott, *A World Waiting To Be Born: Civility Rediscovered*. (Bantam Books: New York, 1993), 40.

48. Gardner, John W, *On Leadership*. (The Free Press: New York, 1990). Hitt, William D., *Ethics and Leadership: Putting Theory into Practice*. (Battelle Press: Columbus, Ohio, 1990. Kouzes, James. M. and Barry Z. Posner, *The Leadership Challenge: How To Get Extraordinary Things Done in Organizations*. (San Francisco: Jossey-Bass, 1987). Kouzes, James. M. and Barry Z. Posner., *Credibility: How Leaders Gain And Lose It, Why People Demand It*. (Jossey-Bass: San Francisco, 1993). Peck, M. Scott, *A World Waiting To Be Born: Civility Rediscovered*. (Bantam Books: New York, 1993). Rosen, Robert with Lisa Berger, *The Healthy Company: Eight Strategies to Develop People, Productivity and Profits*. (Jeremy P. Tarcher/Perigree: New York, 1991). Weisbord, Marvin R., *Productive Workplaces: Organizing and Managing for Dignity, Meaning, and Community*. (Jossey-Bass: San Francisco, 1987).

49. Peck, M. Scott, *The Different Drum: Community-Making and Peace*. Simon and Schuster: (New York, 1987), 118–126. Samuels, Aandrew, et al., A *Critical Dictionary of Jungian Analysis*. (Routledge and Kegan Paul LTD: New York, 1993), 150–151.

50. Wheatley, Margaret. J. and Myron Kellner-Rogers, *A Simpler Way*. (Berrett-Koehler: San Francisco, 1996), 51.

51. Ford, Leighton, Transforming Leadership: Jesus' Way of Creating Vision, Shaping Values and Empowering Change. (InterVarsity Press: Downers Grove, Ill., 1991). Gardiner, John. J. and Beverly A. Forbes. Preparing Effective Leaders For An Interdependent World: Seattle University's Multidisciplinary Doctoral Cohorts. Paper presented to the National Leadership Group of the American Council on Education, Washington, D.C. December 3, 1993. Hess, Hess, Beth B., Elizeabeth W. Markson, and Peter J. Stein, Sociology: Third Edition. MacMillan (Publishing Company: New York, 1988). Hollander, Edwin. P. (1978). *Leadership Dynamics: A Practical Guide to Effective Relationships*. (The Free Press: New York, 1978). Kouzes, James. M. and Barry Z. Posner, *The Leadership Challenge: How To Get Extraordinary Things Done*

in Organizations. (San Francisco: Jossey-Bass, 1987). Kouzes, James. M. and Barry Z. Posner., *Credibility: How Leaders Gain And Lose It, Why People Demand It*. (Jossey-Bass: San Francisco, 1993). Peck, M. Scott, *The Different Drum: Community-Making and Peace*. Simon and Schuster: (New York, 1987). Wheatley, Margaret. J. and Myron Kellner-Rogers, *A Simpler Way*. (Berrett-Koehler: San Francisco, 1996).

52. Burns James M, *Leadership*. (Harper and Row: New York, 1978). Ford, Leighton, *Transforming Leadership: Jesus' Way of Creating Vision, Shaping Values and Empowering Change*. (InterVarsity Press: Downers Grove, Ill., 1991). Peck, M. Scott, *The Different Drum: Community-Making and Peace*. Simon and Schuster: (New York, 1987). Samuels, Aandrew, et al., *A Critical Dictionary of Jungian Analysis*. (Routledge and Kegan Paul LTD: New York, 1993). Wheatley, Margaret. J. and Myron Kellner-Rogers, *A Simpler Way*. (Berrett-Koehler: San Francisco, 1996).

53. Peck, M. Scott, *The Different Drum: Community-Making and Peace*. Simon and Schuster: (New York, 1987), 21.

54. Peck, The Different, Community, 51.

55. Hammond, Joshua and James Morrison. (1996), Stuff Americans Are Made Of: Seven Cultural Forces That Define Americans—A New Framework For Quality, Productivity And Profitability. Simon and Schuster Macmillan Company: New York., 251–255.

56. Peck, M. Scott, *The Different Drum: Community-Making and Peace*. Simon and Schuster: (New York, 1987), 60–66.

57. Peck, The Different, Community, 73–77.

58. Peck, The Different, Community, 75.

59. Peck, The Different, Community, 83–85.

60. Peck, The Different, Community, 87–103.

61. Peck, The Different, Community, 102.

62. Peck, The Different, Community, 109–118.

63. Bolman, Lee G. and Terrence E. Deal, *Reframing Organizations: Artistry, Choice, and Leadership*. (Jossey-Bass: San Francisco, 1991). Kouzes, James. M. and Barry Z. Posner, *Credibility: How Leaders Gain And Lose It, Why People Demand It*. (Jossey-Bass: San Francisco, 1993), Peck, M. Scott, *The Different Drum: Community-Making and Peace*. (Simon and Schuster: New York, 1987), 136–149.

64. Peck, The Different, Community, 55.

65. Peck, The Different, Community, 81.

66. Peck, The Different, Community, 78.

67. Peck, The Different, Community, 69.

68. Peck, The Different, Community, 31–32.

69. Peck, The Different, Community, 65–67.

70. Peck, The Different, Community, 66–72.

71. Peck, The Different, Community, 64–65.

72. Peck, The Different, Community, 72.

73. Peck, The Different, Community, 73–77.

74. Wheatley, Margaret. J. and Myron Kellner-Rogers, *A Simpler Way*. (Berrett-Koehler: San Francisco, 1996), 43.

75. Wheatley, *A Simpler Way*, 20.

76. Wolinsky, Stephen, *Quantum Consciousness: The Guide to Experiencing Quantum Psychology.* (Bramble Books: Northfork, Conn.,1993), 9.

77. Wolinsky, *Quantum Consciousness*, 21.

78. Wolinsky, *Quantum Consciousness*, 25–50.

79. Wolinsky, *Quantum Consciousness*, 52–88.

80. Herbert, Quantum Reality, 1985.

81. Wazlawick, 1984.

82. Wolinsky, *Quantum Consciousness*, 139.

83. Wolinsky, *Quantum Consciousness*, 142–160.

84. Wolinsky, *Quantum Consciousness*, 162–188.

85. Wolinsky, *Quantum Consciousness*, 142–160.

86. Herbert, Quantum Reality, 18–19.

87. Wolinsky, *Quantum Consciousness*, 20.

88. Wolinsky, *Quantum Consciousness*, 20.

89. Herbert, Quantum Reality, 1985.

90. Aziz, 1954; Bellah et al., 1995, 1991; Covey, 1989, 1992; Ford, 1991; Jung, 1973; Greenleaf, 1982; Hall & Thompson, 1980; Kouzes & Posner, 1987, 1993; Peck, 1997; Wheatley, 1992.

91. Herbert, 1985, pp. 146–149.

Chapter Three

Interdisciplinary Reflections on Voice

Because the personal integrity and high standards of many business leaders are so clearly in line with their ideals, the failure of these standards to appear in the outcomes of leadership and proactive management in some of their companies is a puzzling paradox.[92] The paradox of values faced by Chief Executive Officers is the gap between the idea of equal opportunity and the practice of prejudice.

Lewis B Ward

Most people who are bullies, difficult people, or predators immediately spot, react, and effectively stop abusive behaviors at work directed at them. Why? Because regardless of the effect on you bullies, difficult people, and predators will use anything, or do anything at their disposal to get what they want. No behavior is too outrageous to be implemented.

On the other hand, individuals who are repulsed by aggression, or think they are "holding their own," typically miss or deny the first stages of attack from their nemesis. By the time the average person recognizes their job is in jeopardy they may be so overwhelmed that, not only is their reaction slowed, but what they do is too little and too late to be effective to stop their nemesis. Sometimes, for a number of reasons (social, religious, gender, long-standing subjection to abusive relationships) some individuals do not even realize that they have been personally and deliberately targeted by their nemesis at work. So, the question is why would you put up with abusive, often illegal behaviors toward you at work? The reasons may include:

1. You are a person who has been raised to respect authority.
2. You typically give others, especially those in authority, the benefit of the doubt.

3. You have been condition to "keep quite." So at work, this condition carries over. You just do not "tell" what obnoxious and degrading things are happening in your work unit. Besides, no one will pay attention to what you say anyway because no one wants to "hear it."
4. You are afraid that any complaining will jeopardize your job.
5. You have witnessed others who have spoken up be targeted and labeled in derogatory and punitive ways.
6. You realize that everything changes so you figure you'll just wait it out.
7. You figure that this place you work is no better or worse than any other place you could work.
8. You actually love your work, are good at your work and respected—and you refuse to be driven away from your work.

Working in a hostile work environment with one or more nemesis is comparable to going to war daily. Denying you work in a war zone is understandable. To admit you work in a war zone means that you are a combatant, not an employee. And, most of us have not been trained to be a combatant; just good, honest, hard working citizens that give an honest day's work for an honest day's pay.

DISCUSSION OF VISION AND VOICE

One chooses her thoughts moment to moment.[93] Awareness of one's freedom to choose gives the freedom to choose a new thought. Thoughts, also called imagery or described as vision, are the language of the subconscious.[94] One always moves in the direction of his thoughts.[95] Consciously using the visualization process is like using electricity—understanding how electricity works is unnecessary to get results. An individual's "power" is always present. Initiating one's power is unnecessary; only direction is required.[96] The speed with which goals are achieved depends upon how clearly and how often they are visualized.[97] No thought or emotion is without biochemical and electrochemical activity and this activity leaves no cell untouched.[98] Reality is created twice, once in the imagination and then in the world.[99] Events move too fast (in the biochemical and electrochemical activity) for a change in direction to be made while in motion. Therefore, it is necessary for the individual to visualize events exactly as desired before the action/creation of form occurs.[100] Fear destroys perception and manipulates the fearful into creating that which is most feared.[101]

Evolution as survival of the fittest has inhibited our observation of evolution. We are not independent agents pitting for ourselves against all others. There is no hostile world out there plotting our demise. There is no "out there" for anyone to occupy. We are utterly intertwined. Always we are working out condi-

tions for life with others. We play an essential role in shaping each other's behavior. We select certain traits and behaviors. They respond to us. Their response changes us. We are linked together. We co-determine the conditions of
one another's existence. . . . No one forges ahead independently, molding the
world to his or her presence while the rest rail admiringly behind. We tinker ourselves into existence by unobserved interactions with the players who present
themselves to us. Environments, enemies, allies—all are affected by our efforts
as we are by theirs. The systems we create are chosen together. They are the result of dances, not wars.

Wheatley & Kellner-Rogers

VOICE CONGRUENCY AND DISCIPLINE CREATES FORM

Discussion of effective leadership, "good" management, work values/ethics,
productive workforces, and healthy work environments requires a review of
effective communication. Only recently has it been acknowledged that some
types of verbal communication, rather than simply reflecting bad communication skills, are significantly more harmful. Some types of communication,
it is increasingly being recognized, may in fact be abusive communication.[102]

The recognition of verbal abuse, although increasing, tends to focus on personal relationships. Scant research or recognition of the cost of verbal abuse
in the workforce has occurred.

The preponderance of the literature to date recognizes verbal abuse as a legitimate, distinguishable form of psychological exploitation and brutality. Effective leaders and "good" managers envision, form, and sustain productive
and healthy work environments, with communication skills being an essential
component of accomplishing their objectives. An overview of the literature
that specifically relates to leadership, organizational development, and management reveals that, while communication is much discussed, the closest acknowledgment of psychological abuse is limited to the areas of fear, discrimination, self-esteem/morale, self-fulfilling prophecy, or "looking-glass"
assessments.[103]

FEAR

Both Ryan and Oestreich (1991) in *Driving Fear Out of the Workplace* and
Denim's eighth point in his continuous quality control model[104] encourage effective two-way communication and hint at "bad" communication. According
to their models, closed or bad communication results in poor team spirit and
cooperation as well as "workplace fear."

DISCRIMINATION

Both Cox's (1993) *Cultural Diversity in Organizations* and Bass's (1990) *Bass and Stodill's Handbook of Leadership* allude to verbal abuse in the workplace, but only those readers sophisticated and seasoned in Civil Rights typically clearly and immediately comprehend that discrimination and harassment are inherent outcomes of verbal abuse. Many who have reflected[105] on communication proficiency all converge on the same indicators and outcomes of verbal abuse: various forms of discrimination and harassment, prejudice and discrimination, stereotyping and instigating conflict among and between groups.

Hall and Thompson (1980) and Maslow (1993[106]) link communication with self-definition and the fulfillment of human needs. Rather than fulfilling human needs, as iterated in Maslow's hierarchy (basic physical needs, safety, social, self-esteem, and self-actualization) or expanding Hall and Thompson's leadership level of consciousness, within the leadership or management relationship, verbally abusive communication derives from Machiavellian paradigm.[107]

Machiavellian tactics, as delineated in *The Prince* (1513), assume that power is an end in itself and is separate from morality, ethics, religion, and metaphysics. The "state" (which can be extrapolated to any person in authority) is viewed as an autonomous system of values independent of any other source. This value system may in fact violate other value systems, but when performed pursuant to the "reason of the state," acts may be permissible, and even obligatory, although in other value "systems" such acts would be considered heinous crimes.

Those guided by the "reason of the state" are guided solely by the precept that the "end" or goal is the acquisition, retention, and expansion of power, thus one of Machiavelli's most famous quotes: "in the actions of the rulers the end justifies the means." In such a paradigm, good and evil are reduced from absolute to relative categories; the determination of whether an act is good or evil depends entirely on the basic assumption of one's system of values. If the basic or core value is assuming and maintaining power, then assuming power, regardless of the means used, is good. The means of acquiring, consolidating, and expanding power are good as long s they accomplish their task, as long s they are efficient. Therefore, utilizing efficient means is "good," and use of any inefficient means is "bad",[108] regardless of the insult or harm to coworkers, subordinates, or others with whom one comes in contact through his position of power.

There is agreement[109] that power, in the sense of domination over others, is excessive assertion. In the "traditional," hierarchical organization, many men and women equate or integrate their position in the organizational hierarchy with their identity. If a leader or manager has associated their personal identity with their position within the hierarchy, then a shift to a different system of values provokes fear. It is clear that there is another kind of power, one that influences others, which sustains its potency and authority from networks, not hierarchical composition.[110]

Rubin's *The Princessa: Machiavelli for Women* (1997), views power as the ability to combine opposites, which is key too not "playing by the rules." Rubin defines "Princessa" as literally meaning "she who takes first place," which she states is an anglicized form of the Italian principessa, derived from "principle" and "excellence." Like Forbes (1991) and Gilligan (1993), Rubin asserts that there are (most generally attributed to) feminine characteristics or traits of sensitivity, emotional depth, selflessness, and the tendency to be peacemakers, caretakers and nurturers could be advantageous as the paradigms regarding work and interrelatedness change. Rubin contends that the woman who governs by principles not laws is usually underestimated and most often invisible, until recently. The Princessa's advice to women, to live their lives as people for whom triumph is a birthright, may be extrapolated to be gender neutral if "triumph" is defined as one's awakening to awareness. It is at this juncture that Rubin's concepts would merge with Capra's (1996) that one does not have to choose between opposites such as love and power.

SELF-ESTEEM/MORALE

Burns insinuates that effective leaders and "good" managers not only form and sustain productivity and healthy work environments with good communication skills, but that a leader's verbally abusive communications to others may be an indication of the leader's petty quest for esteem and prestige. Burns contends that the individual's need for affection and belonging is powerful, and when these needs are combined with the effects of social influences, political forces tend to produce various forms of leadership. He states: "leadership becomes a matter of all-too-human motivation and goals, of conflict and competition that seems to be dominated by the petty quest for esteem and prestige."[111] Burns' cautions are an important reminder that leadership is intensely individual and personal.

Similarly, Bass (1990) contains considerable discussion regarding self-esteem and leadership, showing that:

1. Self-esteem tends to be higher in leaders/managers than in their followers.
2. A positive relationship exists between self-esteem and leadership.

3. Persons who feel personally accepted or esteemed tend to exhibit greater leadership.
4. Persons with high self-esteem are more likely to attempt leadership.
5. Leaders with high self-esteem are likely to transfer high self-esteem to their followers.

The fifth point holds important implications: a leader with high self-esteem, and who is willing and able to transfer high self-esteem to her followers, can perform without having to resort to criticism or negative reinforcement. Self-esteem in leaders appears to be related to being able to: (a) accept people as they are; (b) focus on the present; (c) be courteous to both colleagues and strangers; (d) trust others; and (e) to resist the need for constant approval and recognition. The significant implications of verbal abuse on one's self-esteem/morale are comparable to the negative effects of verbal abuse on leadership and on follower's productivity.

SELF-FULFILLING PROPHECY/PYGMALION EFFECT

Leighton Ford's discussion in *Transforming Leadership* (1991) of the leader as spokesperson and Covey's deliberation in *Seven Habits of Highly Effective People* (1989) regarding "listening to our language,"[112] review the importance of effective communication skills. These two authors indirectly chastise verbal abuse in the workplace by emphasizing the significance of the self-fulfilling prophecy. Both Bass (1990) and Kreitner and Kinicki (1992[113]) point out the significance of the "Pygmalion effect"[114] within organizations: the tendency for increased levels of achievement and productivity to coincide with a manager's rising expectation for individuals performing job tasks, so;

• high supervisory expectancy produces better leadership,
• which leads employees to develop higher self-expectations,
• which motivate workers to exert more effort.
• Life's like this which ultimately increase performance and supervisory expectancies.

Additionally, successful performance also improves as an employee's self-expectancy for achievement[115] increases. Thus, a continuous self-fulfilling, self-expectancy cycle is established and continues until some significant intervention breaks the cycle. Therefore, largely due to the Pygmalion effect, Kreitner and Kinicki, as does Bass, conclude that the expectations of the leaders and managers powerfully influence the employee's behavior and performance.

One of the fundamental principles of leadership and management is that constructive comments or communications are necessary to realize positive performance expectations. The significant implications of the Pygmalion effect concerning this research are the strongly suggested negative effects of verbal abuse in the work environment for both the leader and the employees.

LOOKING GLASS EFFECT

Hess et al. (1988) suggests that each of us has a basic self-feeling that is shaped and given content through our interactions with others. Over time we develop a self-concept that matches the way we believe that others see us, particularly those we perceive to be important, significant, or as having "power over" us. This process has formidable impact on both the development and perpetuation of our self-concept.[116] The literature concurs that we tend to accept impressions that reinforce our basic identity and tend to resist those that do not, unless there is a significant emotional event that alters the basic self-concept.

The significance of an individual's self-concept/self-esteem in organizations is (or should be) of tremendous importance to managers. Kreitner and Knicki's (1992) study of organization-based self-esteem, which has been validated with seven other studies, defined organization-based self-esteem as "the self-perceived value that individuals have of themselves as organization members acting within an organizational context." That study found that active enhancement of organization-based self-esteem tends to build a very important cognitive bridge to greater productivity and satisfaction.

VERBAL ABUSE

Patricia Evans (1992, 1993, 2002) and Jennifer James (1987, 1990) have done the most extensive work in the field of verbal abuse, with their emphasis primarily contained to personal relationships. Evans point out that the majority of us are beginning to understand that name-calling is verbally abusive. However, equally disparaging forms of verbal abuse, often disguised rather than blatant, include being told in subtle or not-so subtle ways that:

- One's perception of reality is wrong.
- One's ability to think or reason is wrong.
- One's feelings are wrong.
- One's interests are wrong.
- One's presence is rejected.

Verbal abuse is experiential in nature, escalating over time, often occurring in a one-to-one encounter with the abuser denying the abuse (Evans 1992, 1993). Verbal abuse can occur through several demeanors, including:

- Countering
- Criticizing
- Discounting
- Forgetting
- Intimidating
- Manipulating
- Name-calling
- Sarcasm
- Trivializing
- Undermining
- Withholding

Verbal abuse may be overt or covert and is hostile aggression that generally must be recognized by the recipient because the abuser is not motivated to change. If and when the recipient shares her feelings with the abuser, it is absolutely certain the abuser will invalidate her.[117] This type of prolonged, escalating encounter is "crazy-making" to the recipient.[118] The recipient "learns" to tolerate the abuse, often without realizing it and to loose self-esteem, usually without realizing that the experiences are abusive. She loses self-esteem, usually without realizing the self-change she is undergoing. Verbal abuse, by its very nature, undermines and discounts its victim's perceptions. Verbal abuse always takes its toll without respect to gender.

"We can accept a leader who is demanding but not one who is demeaning."

Joyce James

As James points out, verbal abuse was functional when survival depended on stoicism, fear, and no-questions-asked physical responses. However, the new paradigm of relationships requires a new verbal awareness, grace, and sensitivity.

Verbal abuse is based in the abuser's need to have "power over" someone, to control another's behavior.

Patricia Evans

"Power" in relationships can be considered from two primary models: "power over" and "personal power."[119] Western civilization was founded on the "power over" model, which is displayed as control and dominance, killing the other's spirit. The aggressor is motivated to control and dominate others to support her illusion of power, which is maintained only as long as she has an "other" to have power over.[120]

The arena of work is a culture perfectly structured to foster and sustain a verbal abuser. Evans' identification of the ten overt or covert indicators of verbal abuse is analogous to Bass' depiction of Machiavellian tactics in leadership and management. The cost, in terms of productivity and profit resulting from verbal abuse in incalculable, however some of the toll may be seen in:

- personnel turnover,
- recruitment and training retention expenditures,
- labor disputes,
- formal and informal disciplinary actions and litigation fees,
- loss of enthusiasm by individuals, teams, or groups,
- hesitancy or refusal to take risks, and
- reluctance to come to conclusions. The frequency and pervasiveness with which verbal abuse occurs irrespective of work and income are stunning.

Peck (1993) postulates that by the time a person reaches a position of leadership or senior management, his heart will belong either to personal ambition or to his spiritual tenets. If the leader's heart "belongs" to ambition, then his primary considerations will be the politics of the situation, his popularity, and instituting cosmetic "fixes" to issues. On the other hand, if the leader's heart "belongs" to his spiritual tenets, then his primary consideration will be to what is "right." The perpetuation or toleration of verbal abuse and its subsequent "cost" are directly proportionate to who the abuser is and the values of the leader.

This work contends that if the leader or manager is aware that his voice creates form, then he will ensure that those to whom he has delegated administrative authority do not disrupt the form he desires. He will ensure that the transmission of his voice is delegated to one who can also transmit the form he desires. Figure 3.1, depicts the interdependence of a transformational leader's consciousness, subconscious and socialization. In every instance, the leader's core values manifest in the leader's environment "who" and "what" she "is."

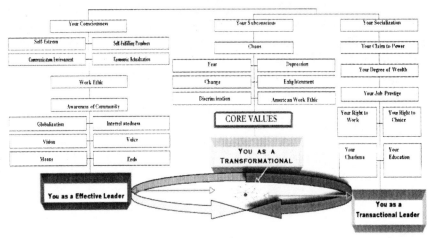

Figure 3.1.   Transformational Leader's Consciousness.

ARE YOU A BULLY, DIFFICULT PERSON, OR A PREDATOR

> When two quantum entities, A and B, briefly interact (via conventional local forces) then move apart beyond the range of initial interaction, quantum theory does not describe them as separate objects, but continues to regard them as a single entity. If one takes seriously this feature, called quantum inseparability, then all objects that have once interacted are in some sense still connected.
>
> Nick Herbert

What specifically makes a person "difficult," a "bully," a "predator"? Or perhaps a more answerable question might be what differentiates a "difficult person" from a "bully," from a "predator"? Typically the answer to this question is the degree of orneriness, as we perceive the individual's behaviors. The individual's "unreasonableness" when coupled with the individuals authorized and/or informal authority and power over us may pose the paradox of submit to the power and work, resist and be unemployed. The stereotyped predatory personality is one of a detestable person who is easily recognizable. However typically excluded, sometimes contrary to all evidence, is the likable person; the nice person as being a "bully", "determinedly difficult", or a "predator." Contemporary research by both Robert Hare (1993) and Anna Salter (2003) rigorously caution us that "niceness" and "likability" are decisions each person makes, these behaviors are not character traits. Particularly with predators their superficial charisma may conceal their deception, duplicity, and disloyalty. So now this is a puzzle, the difficult person can be the irritating to just "plain mean" individual that you have no trouble identifying or she could be the "nice", "likable" person whom you trust and respect. The span of detrimental character flaws pretty much includes everyone, so what do you do to keep from becoming paranoid?

Sometimes experience softens the edges of skepticism and sharpens the murky focus of innocence. Patrick Grim (2005) emphasizes the importance of distinguishing the difference between a "fact" and one's values. The confusion all of us tend to make at some time is between what "ought to be," from what "is". There can be the all to common inference "automatically" made that a person's "behaviors" are equivalent to that person's "character." This presumption of one's behavior being equivalent to one's character has all too often resulted in our making unpleasant if not terrible decisions. Our emotional maturity develops along with our self-appreciation as we begin to comprehend that some people are as repelled to consideration of others (with about as much feeling too) as two magnets have the capacity to repel each other.

Some of us have been around an individual or a group of people who leave us disoriented, feeling unbalanced, disconnected, or just plain "bugged" by that person or environment but we just can not seem to explain why. And, oddly enough many of us tend to discount any feeling that we can not logically explain so we remain in the situation ignoring all the clues that something is very wrong. Many of us have worked in an environment where there is an illusion of authentic leadership, however, the reality is a work environment riddled with inequity, competition, manipulation, hostility, control, and negation. In this environment there will never be equality, partnership, mutuality, good will, intimacy, validation, and productivity because either you, your co-worker, or someone in your management chain of command is the bully, determinedly difficult person, or predator. Yet for the sake of the money we habitually compromise our mental health, physical well being, and ultimately our career competencies frantically continuing our death grip on our job's dissolving stability.

The power plays inherent in the work force excrete tangible wealth, status, and the ability to influence others. With these very real, very coveted trappings of accomplishments and victory any and every type of competitor, predator, and adventurer stalks the work force to survive and thrive. The phrase "survival of the fittest" in today's workforce requires that we know what kind of person(s) we are dealing with by removing self-imposed blinders and keeping our emotional guard up. Co-worker and management alliances often change, as do organizational configurations, so office social intimacies can expose your vulnerabilities. Comprehending that co-workers are not your personal friends, they are acquaintances, even the "nice" ones; is essential. Conversely, your realistic self-assessment of the congruency between your values, behaviors, and associations may reveal the discrepancy, if any, between your self-image and your ability to irritate others.

There are several reasons, other than redemptive change, that you might be interested in determining whether or not you are a bully, difficult person, or a predator. These benefits include, but are not limited to unscrupulous power over others, social relationship obliviousness, and unrestrained ego inflation. The characteristics of capitalistic profitability tend to reward egocentric behavior with: attention, position, obedience, and money.[121] So, other than looking in a mirror and being unable to see your reflection (that is if you have mirrors or you actually look in the ones you have), just what indicators are there that you are someone's nemesis?

- Your operative principle is that you have to "go along to get along."
- Your operative principle is that you "can not trust anyone."
- Your operative principle is that you will do "whatever is necessary" to get what you want.
- Your operative principle is "follow the money."
- Your operative principle is that people fit into one of two categories, the users and the used.
- Your operative principle is that in life there are winners and looser and if you are not winning you are loosing.
- Your operative principle is the assumption of arrogance, naturally based on your personal superiority.

If there are such compelling benefits to being a "difficult person," why would you even want to consider changing? Why is making the concerted effort and the resulting confusion of family, friends, and co-workers worth transforming? Because as you begin to transform you will attract serendipity, abundance in all things, and your internal and external Voice will manifest the productive, healthy work place where you will thrive, and you will use less energy doing so—and you will get more money. Also, you always attract what and who you are. In other words, you will quit being drawn toward and being appealing to other bullies, difficult people, and predators. And no, you will not become the prey because you will have the core values, proactive management principles, and consciousness to manifest both effective defensive maneuvers and prosperity.[122]

NOW THAT YOU ARE AWARE: IT IS YOUR MOVE

Nothing happens, until something moves.

Albert Einstein

Arguably, for purest, there is only one consciousness and each of us, regardless of our awareness, comprises part of the whole. Operationally, at least in the world of work, there is the persistent illusion that there are at least two operative consciousnesses; yours and the other person's. When your view of the other person's behaviors toward you is coupled with the degree of potential or actual harm this person poses to your career and livelihood, your perception of this individual's conscious awareness is corrupted. Your realization that your perception of your nemesis (the bully, determinedly difficult person or worse yet predator) is important because your perception, right or wrong, is tainted and thus may adversely impact your judgment and ability to successfully resolve your problem. What you must remember when considering how you are going to resolve your problem is that you must be the first one to change. Why? Because your nemesis is your problem: others are relieved she is focused on you, and they do not have a problem. Your nemesis is having a good day regardless of your presence and therefore is not even considering changing.

The most difficult part of needing to be the first one to change is not necessarily wounding your pride. Your ability to comprehend why you have to change first will be determined by how long it takes for you to understand that it is you that has been "wronged." Since you are the one that's been "wronged," you are the one experiencing the tremendous energy drain and your whining poses and increasingly strain on your relationships: between you and your family and friends. The most difficult part of initiating your change is whether or not your self-assessment of your personality, your resources, your rights, and your desired outcome is accurate and obtainable. A hint consider the following: if you started your job as a complete balanced person, the ultimate objective is to remain in your job, or leave your job (whenever that happens and however that happens), a complete balanced person.

Your Personality

Ultimately, what is important about your personality is your amount of personal self-esteem, self-discipline, authenticity, and the accuracy of your perceptions of your work situation and your nemesis. This is a time when whether or not you have family/friends, and the quality of your family/friend's judgment will be of critical importance. Why? Because typically your family and friends are the first people you turn to, so they hear from you about the developing friction between you and your nemesis. And, with either "coaching" or "egging," your family/friends typically help you make your decisions regarding how you are going to react to the situations resulting from your ostracism and/or mistreatment at work.

This initial realization that you are the prey for your nemesis requires that you evaluate two critical factors:

1. If you are right and you have a nemesis this person will not stop because you are being provoked, abused, or treated unequally, and
2. It is always easier to escalate your defensive actions than deescalate.

Your nemesis is not an individual with whom you have occasional squabbles. If you are right and you have become the prey for your nemesis, you may be in for an extended period of (politically and/or legally) redirecting the inappropriate behaviors and asserting your right to work in a healthy work environment. This engagement with behavioral changes in both yourself, your nemesis, and your teamwork with management and/or your legal representative will draw upon your personal self-esteem, self-discipline, and character strengths. Why? Because the more your nemesis approaches being your predator the more you will be going it alone (with only your labor representative, attorney, or other counsel).

Know this, once you have your "support and defense" team in place, if you are playing to win your team must be small, may decrease membership over time, and must be able to maintain confidentiality. You will need to be very weary if "all of a sudden" someone wants to join your team to "help" you. Why? Because once you have your defense team in place, new members (intentionally or not), typically derail your strategy and your ultimate ability to win.

Your Resources

Your most prized and basic resource is your health, both mental and physical. If your perceptions are correct and you do have a nemesis the worse thing you can do to hurt your ability to correct the inappropriate behavior(s) or win your legal battle is to act in a rash manner. Inappropriate behaviors, displays of temper, and slipping into poor performance are advantageous to management. Misconduct and/or poor performance allows management to document that you have assumed at least some of the responsibility and that you are contributing to what you are claiming is a hostile work environment. Remember it is your burden of proof that your nemesis has done something wrong to you, caused you harm, and that your work productivity and efficiency has suffered because of how you have been treated. Your mental, emotional, and physical systems are interconnected and how you react will have long-range affects on your health and well being. So first make sure that even if you never considered eating, sleeping, and exercising correctly before; now is the time this regime must be put into place. If you are a spiritual person you will need a place and time each day to reflect and maintain your balance. Why? Because your nemesis is at work and neither work nor your nemesis is your life. So, do not let your entire life be affected by the bully, determinedly difficult person or predator at work. The ability to be perceptive without being penetrated by the devastating behaviors of your nemesis is easier said than done, but this is where self-discipline is indispensable.

Next you need to consider how objective and accurate you are about your situation. If you are both objective and accurate then you will need to consider how you are going to document, retain, and secure evidence supporting your contentions that you are being treated differently, discriminated against, or harassed and how management is contributing to sustaining the hostile work environment. A hint, it is not wise or safe to keep these documents at work or to e-mail yourself from a work location with your supporting documentation. Remember e-mail means "everyone's mail"—there is no privacy of e-mail at work.

A third consideration is what rights, rules and regulations does your place of employment have governing employees? Are you covered by a labor collective bargaining agreement? Are you a permanent, full time employee? If not does temporary or full time employment status make a difference at your place of employment? If you do not know the answer to these questions then you need to find your human resource (personnel) office and ask for copies of all relevant rules, policies, procedures, and contracts that govern your employment. If you are covered by a collective bargaining agreement, or even if you are a dues paying member but are not covered by an agreement then your best, first bet, is to make an appointment with your shop steward and/or paid labor representative. If you are not a member of a labor organization (or even if you are) you will want to meet with your human resource (personnel) manager and discuss your concerns (yes you can take your representative with you for this discussion). But remember when talking with your human resource manager that:

1. A competent human resource manager should be neutral when hearing your complaint/concerns but they may have to ask some very specific questions. Of course your human resource manager will be talking with management about your concerns—but then you want them to.
2. A competent human resource manager will always give you your rights (company policies, procedures, and state and Federal laws). If you have concerns regarding discrimination, harassment, your employer's failure to accommodate, have issues about leave which may be covered by Labor and Industries claims, Family Medical Leave Act, and types of authorized leave without pay; then your human resource manager is a necessary contact point.

3. A competent human resource manager will always ask you if you are covered by a labor collective bargaining agreement and remind you that you have the right to representation should you desire. (What those rights are will of course be determined by the contract.)
4. A competent human resource manager will remain neutral in her advice to both you and management. Should your concerns escalate to the point where you have some type of outside appeal (mediation, arbitration, lawsuit, outside discrimination/harassment complaint), your human resource manager should be telling you that you need to seek a personal representative (labor/attorney/fiend). From this point on your human resource manager will be representing management.

Next, you are going to want to acquaint yourself, if you do not know already, with what your employer's policies, labor Collective Bargaining Agreement, state and Federal laws and recent court decisions are in the following areas. One or more of these areas may provide some protection or rights in your particular situation or from your nemesis.

- Abandonment of (your) Position
- Access to your medical file (should be separate from personnel file)
- Access to your personnel file
- Access to your reasonable accommodation file (should be separate from personnel file)
- Constructive discharge (if you felt compelled to quit)
- Contracting out/outsourcing (your job)
- Corrective Action (definition of)
- Disability Separation (both voluntary and involuntary)
- Disciplinary Action (definition of)
- Discrimination (prevention)
- Domestic Violence
- Hostile Work Environment (definition of)
- Insubordination
- Misconduct (definition of)
- On the job injuries
- Process and Procedures (for your) Involuntary Termination
- Public Disclosure of Information
- Reasonable Accommodation
- Retaliation
- Sexual Harassment (prevention)
- Substance Abuse
- Violence in the Workplace

In addition to the rights and protections afforded by your employer and/or collectively bargained labor contract, you may also want to know what Federal and/or State Civil Rights laws may have been violated by the actions, omissions that may constitute discrimination, harassment, and/or retaliation. The following overview of legislation that protects employees is provided as only a sampling of protective laws. Additionally, the brief description about each law is in no way intended to be inclusive of the law in its entirety, subsequent case law in the areas, or precedent from employment Arbitration decisions. If you feel you/your job is in jeopardy, you must contact either your human resources manager, equal employment officer, labor representative, attorney, or your state's Human Rights Office. Take any and all documents you have so that together you can review any law updates, any distinguishing characteristics unique to your situation to ferret out "management rights," hostile working conditions, discrimination, harassment, and retaliation as it may relate to you. With this said, you may want to consider some of the following federal legislation[1][2][3] presented in the following Table 1, when considering your options if you choose to legally confront your nemesis.

Finally, you are going to need to consider your tangible assets. Not just your bank account (or lack of one) but your ability to use transferable work knowledge, skills, and abilities to go to allied work opportunities so that you can financially maintain yourself and your family if you get fired, quit, or voluntarily demote to some other job. When you realize you have options then your stress level drops, your negotiation capabilities increase, and your political power increases. Just remember that even if you quit and get another job, after the "honeymoon" if you work with five or more people there is a very good a chance you'll be prey at this new job. This is not said to depress you, just to remind you that what you want as the solution to your "problem" with your nemesis is probably more important than how dastardly your nemesis has acted toward you. Why? Because another person will never be able to "feel" your pain so revenge just will not happen. Also, if you ask for something you can actually achieve, get it, "win" and move on; you'll be able to promote out of this "compost environment."

Your Rights

In the workplace discretion often is the better part of working by the "letter of one's rights" when looking at coexisting in your workplace community. Some of you reading this book are the bully, difficult person, or predator but like vampires you do not see your reflection in the despair, unmotivated, high absenteeism, or low productivity of your subordinates and/or co-workers. And yes, it is possible to be both victim of your nemesis—and—also to be the nemesis of someone else.

Table 1.   Employment Laws Your Nemesis May Have Violated in Her Treatment of You

Does This Apply To You?	*Basic Overview of Law*
Age Discrimination Act	Prohibits discrimination in employment for individuals 40 and over, except where age is a Bona Fide Occupational Qualification (BFOQ).
American with Disabilities Act (ADA)	Prohibits discrimination against qualified individuals (with actual or perceived) disabilities in the recruitment, hiring, training, and retention of their jobs. Individuals must be able to perform the essential functions of their job with or without a reasonable accommodation.
Civil Rights Act of 1991	Increases for victims of intentional discrimination (by employers or their agents) the damage awards. Victims have the right to a trial by jury and jury awards may include compensatory as well as punitive damages.
Congressional Accountability Act	Requires all federal employee relations' legislation enacted by Congress must apply to employees of Congress.
Employer Polygraph Protection Act of 1988	Provides protection for current and prospective employees form lie detector tests or other mechanical or electrical devices. There are exclusions from this protection for some "security sensitive" positions.
Executive Orders (Federal) 11246, 11375, 11478, and 12138	Federal contractors and subcontractors with contracts exceeding $10,000 during any 12-month period, must make affirmative, meaningful action to eliminate artificial barriers to women and minorities—in recruitment, hiring, training, and maintaining women and minorities.
Fair Labor Standards Act of 1938	Establishes regulations for hourly and salaried employees regarding base pay, overtime pay, payroll record keeping, and other terms of employment compensation.
Family Medical Leave Act of 1993	Applies to employers with at least 50 employees in 75-mile radius regarding job secrete/retention during certain types of illnesses. Addresses both chronic and intermittent illnesses for the employee and certain family members.
Immigration Reform and Control Act.	Prohibits discrimination against job applicants on the basis of national origin, citizenship, and ethnicity. Establishes penalties against employers for hiring illegal aliens and requires employers to verify each employee's identity and eligibility to work within three days of being hired.
Occupational Safety and Health Act (OSHA) of 1970	Applies to employers with at least 10 employees, exceptions may include family farms worked only by family members and self-employed workers. In general this law assists and monitors employers in their providing an effective program for enforcement (and reporting of) safety and health standards.
Pregnancy Discrimination Act	Amended Title VII to include prohibition against discrimination on the basis of pregnancy, childbirth, or related conditions. Employers are required to treat pregnancy the same as any other temporary disability.

Table 1.   *(continued)*

Does This Apply To You?	Basic Overview of Law
Privacy Act of 1974	This act addresses the protection and privacy of your personal personal information. This law requires that a government entity must have your signature in order to release its information about you to someone else.
Rehabilitation Act	Applies only to employers who have contracts with the federal government or federal contractors with contracts over $10,000. This act prohibits discrimination based on physical or mental disabilities and unless there is a undue hardship on the employer, the employer must make reasonable accommodations so the individual may do the jobs essential functions.
Title VII of the Civil Rights Act of 1964	Prohibits discrimination, segregation, retaliation based on color, national origin, race, religion, sex.
Vietnam Era Veterans Readjustment Assistance Act	Federal and State governments, and employers with federal contracts are prohibited against discriminating against certain veterans in recruitment, hiring, training, and sustaining their employment.
Worker Adjustment and Retraining Notification Act	Requires some employers to give a minimum of 60 days notice if a plant is to close or if mass layoffs are pending.

Having said this, what are your rights other than those expressed in your work place policies, state, and Federal laws? You have the right, regardless how reasonably eccentric you are, to be tolerated (not necessarily accepted) in the work place so that you and everyone can perform your jobs. No, your co-workers don't have to like you enough to date you or adopt you (or even eat lunch with you), just respectability tolerate you so you all can get your job done. Remember if you really are out of place, you are not an indentured slave, you can and probably should find another work environment. If you are correct and you really do not "fit," then you must realize that you have a very good chance of being someone else's nemesis. Yes, you may be the reason someone is reading this book. Do you realize that regardless of your competence and productivity; the other part of your ability to remain gainfully employed is your "maintenance" factor. If you are difficult person to "maintain" then you are costing management more to keep you than to get rid of you. A valuable employee (to management) is one that is worth more to keep working than to maintain. So, yes your behavior and attitude are observable, objectively quantifiable and will be evaluated (as either misconduct and/or poor performance) along with your work excellence, productivity, knowledge, skills, and abilities.

If however, you are being subjected to abuse, disparate treatment, harassment, retaliation, or management's failure to reasonably accommodate you, seek legal advice and take action. Rights are no good if you do not exercise them or they are striped from you. Remember, in the case of discrimination complaints (best filed with the Federal Equal Employment Opportunity Commission) you have 180 days (6 months) from the most recent act/omission of discrimination, harassment, or retaliation. Check with an attorney to determine whether or not, and when, you can file a criminal and/or civil suit against your employer and/or any individual employee acting on behalf of your employer.

Your Desired Outcome(s)

Knowing what you want, wanting what you asked for, and knowing when to settle are the key to sustain survival and promotions in the workplace. Typically, asking management to fire your supervisor or the menacing co-worker will not happen. And, even if it does management will wait long enough to do it so that you will most probably not be able to say your actions caused her firing. Another thing to keep in mind is that asking for management to apologize or transfer you—for some reason is like asking them to tap dance on a grain of rice. It may happen, but the rice is ground into dust. So, what do you ask for? Well, in most cases (especially when the inappropriate behavior first starts) what you most want is for the inappropriate behavior to stop. So, tell management that. If you are a "control freak," then you may want to specifically stipulate how management is going to get your nemesis to stop. Perhaps you even want them trained in some way. Well, go ahead and say this if it really makes you feel better. Just remember that you will spend more effort on "monitoring" for self-satisfaction than you will on "getting on" with your work life and next promotion. All you should care about is that your nemesis stops messing with you. Trust me, if your nemesis is really a bully, determinedly difficult person, or a predator your getting management to make him stop will be horrific, in the mind of your nemesis. So, your most powerful request for resolution to your problem is to tell management that you want them to stop your nemesis' unauthorized and inappropriate behavior.

When you go to management (your immediate supervisor, someone in your chain of command, or your human resource (personnel) manager you will need to specifically tell them the problem. General statements of dissatisfaction, feeling uncomfortable, or being irritated that the person is alive and breathing in your space will be insufficient to get a response from management. When you can specifically describe the incident, give a date, time, place, and whether or not there are any witnesses or other forms of documentation you will immediately get management's attention. It is always in your best interest to attempt to resolve your concerns, initially, at the lowest administrative level possible. Too shy to speak up, then go with your representative and they will express your concerns. Or, write your concerns (in this case e-mail is OK) to management.

Whether you verbally tell or state your concerns in writing you have to let management know at least once you are experiencing difficulties—and what would in your mind resolve those difficulties. After you have notified management, keep as part of your documentation:

* who in management you notified,
* when, how, and what you said when you notified them,
* what if anything happened after you notified management; and
* what harm you suffered.

The following Figure 3.2, is a worksheet for you to collect your thoughts, putting them in a comprehensible order for someone not familiar with your situation. Answering each of these questions may take a bit of time and effort. However, after you have answered these questions and you have gathered the appropriate documentation (if any exists) you and your counsel will have a realistic assessment of what type of case you have, if you do have one. Taking the time to go through the following work sheet each and every time you are verbally abused and/or treated differently than others is important. Why? Because if you "just complain" to your supervisor, human resource manager, file a grievance, file a discrimination/harassment complaint, or file some type of lawsuit; you will be the one making the charges that you have received disparate treatment, and/or have been the target of retaliation. So, you will be the one who will have to prove your accusations against the bully, determinedly difficult person and/or predator.

Going through the process of completing the worksheet presented in Figure 3.2, is your first step of crucial documentation. For each and every incident you will need to fill one of these worksheets out. Yes, this is a lot of work and requires details and the saving of documents. However, if you expect fair treatment, equally, and civility at work it is going to take more than just your "simple statements" to show that you are being treated differently than others in the same or similar situation(s). It is at this point that one begins to see the interconnectedness of your awareness, your perception of your nemesis, and the involvement of management in creating and sustaining the work environment. These separate and distinct levels of "awareness" (administrators, managers, the difficult persons, and yours) must—and do—merge in the workforce producing the combined consciousness (work environment) that all can thrive in or must endure. By now you see the multitude of considerations necessary for you to evaluate when deciding what to do each and every time your nemesis and/or one of his minions scathes you.

Developing, implementing, and maintaining a game plan to neutralize your nemesis requires both long and short range planning. It is easy to focus on the need for immediate relief from the pestering and bedevilment continuously bombarding you. Your self-discipline and conviction coupled

Figure 3.2.   Worksheet for Writing a Complaint

BACKGROUND INFORMATION:

1) My name:
2) My current position:
   a) My position at the time of the incident I am reporting if different from current position.
3) Number of years in company?
4) Number of years in this specific job?
5) Name of my current supervisor.
   a) Name of supervisor at time of incident I am reporting if different form current supervisor.
6) Number of years supervised by current supervisor?
   a) Number of years supervised by supervisor at time of this reported incident?
7) List Names of Co-workers (at time of incident being reported) and provide the following information for each:
   a) Race
   b) Age
   c) Gender
   d) Disability?
8) Who if anyone performs the identical job as me (at time of reported incident)?
9) Who if anyone performs a job very similar to me (at time of reported incident)?
10) Covered by a Labor Contract at the time of reported incident?
11) I have talked with my Shop Steward and/or paid Labor Representative? (If so when? Why? What happened?
12) I am full time/ part time?
13) I am a shop steward or officer in my union?
14) I am very active in the union but not a shop steward or officer.
15) My last performance evaluation was?
    a) I was rated in my last performance evaluation as?
16) As I write this today I am feeling?
    a) I am writing this at work, at home, where?
17) I have spoken with my human resource (personnel manager)?
    a) When?
    b) Why?
    c) What happened?
18) I have previously filed a grievance?
    a) When?
    b) About what?
    c) The outcome?
19) I have filed a previous Tort or other type of lawsuit?
    a) When?
    b) Against whom?
    c) Anyone at work know I have filed?
20) Specific Incident of this Complaint?
21) Date of occurrence:
    a) Has this happened before? If so when?
    b) Time of occurrence:
    c) Why am I aware of what time it is?

Figure 3.2. *(continued)*

BACKGROUND INFORMATION:

22) Place of occurrence:
23) Is this a work-related incident?
24) Witnesses? (Please write contact information for each: phone number, e-mail, other.)
25) Did I get written statements from witnesses?
26) What happened?
   a) How I felt?
   b) How I behaved?
   c) How I said what I did. (Crying, shouting, whispered .. what?)
   d) What I did immediately after the incident?
27) If I left the work area did I get permission and/or authorized leave first?
   a) How long did I stay away?
28) Who did I talk with about this? (Friend, co-worker, supervisor, personnel, family, other?)
29) How soon after the incident did I talk to the people listed above?
30) Did this incident impact my job or my ability to get another job?
   a) Another job in the same company?
   b) Another job at a different company?
   c) My ability to transfer within the company to a different supervisor?
   d) How I know that my efforts to leave have been blocked?
31) Because of this incident I have been harmed in the following way(s)? Choose all that apply and explain.
   a) "Black-listed" from other jobs I am applying for.
   b) Denied overtime.
   c) Denied promotion.
   d) Denied requested reasonable accommodation.
   e) Denied training opportunity?
   f) Disciplined in some way?
   g) Essential functions of job changed?
   h) Fired?
   i) Humiliated in front of co-workers and/or others?
   j) Involuntarily required to changed shifts?
   k) Laid-off?
   l) Lost money?
   m) Poor performance evaluation?
   n) Working conditions changed?
   o) Other—explain.
32) Who did this to me?
   a) Immediate supervisor?
   b) Co-worker?
   c) Management (someone in management other than my immediate supervisor)?
   d) Customer?
   e) Client?
33) Do I, prior to this incident, have (or have been accused of by management) a history of either poor performance and/or conduct/disciplinary issues?
   a) Last performance evaluation was poor.

(continued)

Figure 3.2.   *(continued)*

BACKGROUND INFORMATION:

    b) I have received oral reprimands in the last year.
    c) I have received written reprimands in the last year.
    d) I have been suspended from work in the last year.
    e) I have had my pay reduced (as punishment) in the last year.
    f) I have been told that I may be fired in the last year.

34) Do I have any documentation?
    a) Performance evaluations,
    b) Written work standards,
    c) Written official description of my job duties,
    d) E-mail,
    e) Charts,
    f) Memo's,
    g) Timesheets
    h) Anything else?

35) Am I out of any money because of this reported incident? If so how much?

36) Do I have receipts to document the money lost and/or expended?

37) Do I have a doctor's and/or health care provider's written statement restricting any of my work capabilities?

38) Have I missed a lot of work specifically related to this incident? (If so why? Anyone who can corroborate the proximate cause of your missing work to this incident?

39) Has the work missed been with or without pay?
    a) I have had unauthorized leave (with or without pay) in the last year?
    b) If I have missed work due to either a personal illness or family illness, has anyone explained to me my "rights" related to:
    c) The Family Medical Leave Act,
    d) The Family Care Act (if your state has one),
    e) Shared Leave Policy if your company has one,
    f) Coverage under the American's With Disability Act,
    g) Reasonable Accommodation if that's appropriate?
    h) Labor and Industry (L&I) claims if appropriate?

40) Disability separation if appropriate?

41) If so what was discussed and when?

42) Is the time I've missed (if that's occurred) being held against me in some negative way—even after I've brought in the appropriate documentation from my physician and/or health care worker?
    a) If so by whom?
    b) Any statements made by co-workers?

43) Do I have a spouse or other family member that is being harassed, intimidated, or retaliated against in any way because of this incident? If so:
    a) When?
    b) By whom?
    c) How?

44) Has this incident been handled confidentially by management?
    a) If not, describe how the confidentiality around this situation has been compromised.
    b) Desired Remedy?

45) The following will resolved this for me and make me whole.

Figure 3.2. *(continued)*

BACKGROUND INFORMATION:

46) Do I really think I can get this resolution?
   a) If not? Then what is that I can realistically expect that will resolve this issue for me?
47) Who I've told what I want?
   a) When did I tell them?
   b) How did I tell them?
   c) Do I have labor/legal representation?
48) Am I within any timeframes for filing my complaint on this issue?
49) What formal complaint process, if any, have I followed to get my desired results?
   (Grievance, OEO internal complaint, external EEOC complaint, law suit, grievance
   . . . other?)
50) Is Labor backing me?
51) 1) Do I have separate legal counsel?
52) Do my family members/personal friends back me?
   a) How many have I told?
   b) Other?

with dispassionate, meticulous, documentation of events when they occur may test your stamina. Realizing that your emotional, legal, and social support system are not co-workers or other employees necessitates you keep your own confidence. Co-workers will not aid you, they may either be your nemesis or one of the minions, but most likely you co-workers are scurrying to avoid the same strict scrutiny and persecution you are under.

The more your nemesis advances from bully, to difficult person and finally arrives at predator, the more fragmented, dysfunctional, and demoralized your entire work unit. Why? Because predators feed on everyone, particularly their minions who have to spend even more time with the predator than you do. Predators are not afraid of litigation, defeat, or being displaced, only of being denied the hunt and kill. In the predator's mind it really boils down to "kill or be killed" and either way the predator thrives on the "game". Neutralizing your nemesis means remembering that consciousness is never inert. Not all managers are proactive, not all senior executives comprehend that they, along with their values (and the actions of those to whom they have delegated authority) develop and sustain the work environment. The following Table 2 displays the five primary areas you need to consider as you develop, adapt and execute your strategy to neutralize your nemesis and any of her minions. Each of the presented five categories must be considered each time that you face making a decision is critical. Why? Because, each abusive, offensive, harassing or retaliatory occurrence you experience is different. If you presume that because some defensive stance "worked" or did not work the first time it will or will not work this time could be fatal to your surviving and neutralizing your nemesis.

Table 2.   Considerations Affecting Your Strategy to Neutralize Your Nemesis

Your (Work) Character, Behavior	Your Core Resolve Toward Nemisis	Political (Work) Environment	Applicable (Work) Laws	Your Nemisis (and His/Her "Kiss up" Minions)

• Aggressive
• Antagonisti
• Arrogant
• Assertive
• Average
• Complaine
• Confident
• Cynical
• Disruptive
• Historian
• Instigator
• Leach
• Loner
• Loud
• Opportunist
• Passive
• Perfectionist
• Protester
• Radical
• Savior
• Self-important
• Sniveler
• Submissive
• Trailblazer
• Victim
	• Appeal to nemesis' compassion.
	• Challenge the system.
	• Convert nemesis to "normal person."
	• Deal breaker; you "win" or you walk.
	• Destroy your nemesis.
	• Expose nemesis to the world.
	• Get even.
	• It's all about the money.
	• Just get along with your nemesis.
	• Just get another job.
	• Pursue fairness because of principle.
	• Pursue nemesis' prejudicial conduct for moral reasons.
	• Solve the problem.
	• Understand your nemesis.
		• What is the power?
		  - Money
		  - Position
		  - Proximity
		  - Informal
		  - Stakeholders
		• Who has the power?
		  - You
		  - Co-worker
		  - Administrative superior.
		  - Administrative subordinate.
		  - Apparent vacuum.
		• How is power used?
		  - Openly
		  - Secretly
		  - Administratively
		  - Socially
		• "Price" of Redemption
		  - Pay then redeemed.
		  - Takes time to regain redemption.
		  - Once "stained" always doomed.
		  - Unknown
			• City laws
			• Collective Bargaining Agreement
			• County laws
			• Division's Policies and procedures
			• Federal laws
			• Management Rights
			• Organizations written Policies and Procedures
			• Past Practices
			• Specific job requirements associated with job's essential functions.
			• State laws
				• Periodically irritating but generally nice.
				• Deceptively difficult; apathetic, spineless.
				• Difficult person, everybody thinks so.
				• Bully, wants what he/she wants . . . now, "just cause I can."
				• Difficult person, primarily with you.
				• Predator: actively searches for life to destroy it.
				• Sociopath Predator: without conscious, erratic stealth (to establish and sustain fear), destroys life.
				• Satan's spawn—pure evil.

NOTES

92. Ward, Lewis B. (1965). "The Ethics of Executive Selection," *Harvard Business Review*, 43 (2), 6–28.

93. Mapes, James. J., *Quantum Leap Thinking: An Owner's Guide to the Mind.* Dove Books: Beverly Hills, 1996), 123.

94. Mapes, *Quantum Leap*, 127.

95. Mapes, *Quantum Leap*, 130.

96. Mapes, *Quantum Leap*, 139.

97. Mapes, *Quantum Leap*, 140.

98. Mapes, *Quantum Leap*, 138.

99. Mapes, *Quantum Leap*, 141.

100. Mapes, *Quantum Leap*, 142.

101. Mapes, *Quantum Leap*, 155.

102. Evans Patricia, *Verbal Abuse Survivors Speak Out: On Relationship and Recovery.* (Bob Adams, Inc. Holbrook, Mass.,1993). James, Jennifer, *Windows.* Expanded edition. (Newmarket Press: New York, 1987). James, Jennifer, *You Know I Wouldn't Say This If I Didn't Love You: How To Defend Yourself Against Verbal Zaps And Zingers.* Revised, expanded edition of *The Slug Manual: The Rise and Fall of Criticism.* (Newmarket Press: New York, 1990). McKay et al., *How to Communicate: The Ultimate Guide to Improving Your Personal and Professional Relationships.* (MJF Books: New York, 1983).

103. Charles Cooley's (1864–1920) "Looking Glass" study concluded that our ideas of "self" come from how we appear to others, how we think they judge our appearances, and how we feel about all this (Hess et al., 1988, pp. 166–118).

104. Neave, Henry R., *The Deming Dimension.* (SPC Press, Inc.: Knoxville, Tenn., 1991).

105. Bass, Bernard M., Bass and Stogdill's Handbook of Leadership: Theory, Research and Managerial Applications. (The Free Press: New York, 1990). Ebenstein, William, Great Political Thinkers: Plato to the Present. (Fourth edition). (Holt, Rinehart and Winston, Inc.: New York, 1969). Cox, Taylor, Cultural Diversity in Organizations: Theory, Research, and Practice. (Berrett-Koehler Publisher: San Francisco, 1993).

106. Alder, Ronald B. and Neil Towne, *Looking Out/Looking In* (7th ed.). (Harcourt Brace Jovanovich College Publishers: Fla., 1993).

107. Machiavellian tactics, discussed by Ebenstein (1969), were first brought to the foreground by Machiavelli in his book *The Prince* (1513). Initially received as shocking and provocative, Machiavelli's work is one of the few political writings that have entered the general body of world literature.

108. Ebenstein, Great Political, 1969.

109. Capra, Fritjof. *The Web of Life: A New Scientific Understanding of Living Systems.* (Doubleday: New York, 1996). James, Jennifer, *Windows.* Expanded edition. (Newmarket Press: New York, 1987). Evans, Patricia, *The Verbally Abusive Relationship: How to Recognize It and How To Respond.* (Bob Adams, Inc.: Holbrook, Massachusetts, 1992). Evans, Patricia, *Verbal Abuse Survivors Speak Out: On Relationship and Recovery.* (Bob Adams, Inc. Holbrook, Mass., 1993).

110. Capri, Fritjof, The Web of Life: A New Scientific Understanding of Living Systems. (Doubleday: New York, 1996). Ford, Leighton, Transforming Leadership: Jesus' Way of Creating Vision, Shaping Values and Empowering Change. (InterVarsity Press: Downers Grove, Ill., 1991). Forbes, Beverly A. (1991). Profile Of The Leader Of The Future: Origin, Premises, Values And Characteristics Of The Theory F Transformational Leadership Model. Unpublished manuscript. Seattle, Wash., October 1993. Gardiner John. J. and Beverly A. Forbes. Preparing Effective Leaders For An Interdependent World: Seattle University's Multidisciplinary Doctoral Cohorts. Paper presented to the National Leadership Group of the American Council on Education, Washington, D.C. December 3, 1993. Gretz Karl. F. and Steven R. Drozdeck, Empowering Innovative People. (Prous Publishing Company: Chicago, 1992). Johansen Robert and Rob Swigart, Upsizing the Individual In The Downsized Organization: Managing in The Wake Of Reengineering, Globalization, And Overwhelming Technological Change. (Doddison-Wesley Publishing: New York, 1994). Rubin, Harriet, The Princessa: Machiavelli for Women. (Currency: New York, 1997).

111. Burns, James M, *Leadership*. (Harper and Row: New York, 1978), 33.

112. Burns, *Leadership*, 78–79.

113. Burns, Leadership, 145.

114. The Pygmalion effect is said to occur when a person's expectations of an event make the outcome more likely to occur than otherwise might have been true. What helps make the event occur is the expectation that it will (Alder & Towne, 1993). In other words, a person's expectations or beliefs determine his behavior and performance, thus serving to make his expectations come true. We strive to validate our perceptions of reality, no matter how faulty they may be (Kreitner & Kinicki, 1992).

115. Ford, Transforming Leadership, 145.

116. Alder, Looking Out, 1993.

117. Evans, Verbally Abusive, 18–21.

118. Evans, Verbally Abusive, 19.

119. Evans, Patricia, The Verbally Abusive Relationship: How to Recognize It and How To Respond. (Bob Adams, Inc.: Holbrook, Massachusetts, 1992). Evans, Patricia, Verbal Abuse Survivors Speak Out: On Relationship and Recovery. (Bob Adams, Inc. Holbrook, Mass.,1993). James, Jennifer, *Windows*. Expanded edition. (Newmarket Press: New York, 1987). James, Jennifer, *You Know I Wouldn't Say This If I Didn't Love You: How To Defend Yourself Against Verbal Zaps And Zingers*. Revised, expanded edition of *The Slug Manual: The Rise and Fall of Criticism*. (Newmarket Press: New York, 1990).

120. This need to have another to control in order to maintain one's sense of power is particularly interesting when the meaning of "other" is considered.

121. The insatiable need to continuously increase profits coupled with the illusive but coveted ability to gain or maintain a competitive edge compels executives, administrators, and line workers. Today's businesses must embrace technological enhancements, rapidly exchange information, and continuously cut cost. Simultaneously competitive businesses demand from shrinking work forces increased productivity, faster deliver or products and/or services while expecting the develop-

ment of new revenue (including "non-profit businesses) by attracting new customers. These characteristics, essential to any business that wants to survive much less thrive, breeds bullies, determinedly difficult people and predators.

122. Wolinsky, Quantum Consciousness, 1933.

123. You should also always check your state and local legislation. Many states and some local jurisdictions have statutes on their books that are either identical to, or in some cases provide greater protection to you, than the Federal legislation. In some instances, these laws are called "fair employment practices," " anti-discrimination," or "human relations" legislation. Often a good place to start your research is going to your favorite internet search engine and typing in either the law or one of the previous terms.

Chapter Four

Values: Sacred, Spiritual and Cultural

We will change our self if we believe that the change will preserve our self. We are unable to change if we cannot find ourselves in a new version of the world. We must be able to see that who we are will not be available in this new situation. . . . Every change occurs only if we identify with it. We encourage others to change only if we honor who they are now. We ourselves engage in change only as we discover that we might be more of who we are by becoming something different.

Margaret Wheatley and Myron Keller-Rogers

Today's workforce does not look, think, or act like the workforce of the past, nor does it hold the same values, have the same experiences, or pursue the same needs and desires. The workforce has changed significantly from six perspectives; age, gender, culture, education, disabilities and values.[124] Shifts in attitude and values have resulted in a variety of lifestyles, motivations, and choices.[125] Hammond and Morrison's (1996) extensive study of Americans, published in *The Stuff Americans Are Made Of* shows that by far the majority of Americans prefer to: have choices, dream the "impossible dream," want "bigger" and "more," "want it now," are not afraid to make mistakes, value improvisation, and always want to know "what's new."

The proliferation of cultural backgrounds at work brings to the workforce many varieties of values, work ethics, and norms of behavior.[126] Attempts by managers to work together with employees of different backgrounds may be hampered by issues of communication, insensitivity, and ignorance of each other's motivation.[127]

To what or whom do our ethical and moral standards commit us if they are "quite independent" of other people's standards and agenda? Two opposing traditions of individualism one manifested in seeking external success and the

60

other in seeking an inward feeling of comfortableness and authenticity ground our self-approval. "Values" are in themselves no answer to shaping moral character, defining limits or determining the community served. "Values," as an isolated concept, turns out to be incomprehensible and rationally indefensible when the ideals of "self" expand or become unencumbered.[128]

Values (along with the individual's self-concept) define what people want from their employment.[129] Values help bring about the kind of business behaviors and principles necessary to stay competitive.[130] Values are where the "hard stuff" and the "soft stuff" come together. Today, to work effectively requires a whole new set of attitudes and behavior. The passivity and dependency of traditional leadership paternalism, doing what one is told, does not work any more. People have to take responsibility, show initiative, be accountable for their own success—and—realize that personal success is interwoven with the success of others.

In return for an employee's greater personal accountability, the company, as a whole, has to communicate more frequently and effectively with both its employees and customers. If there is to be open dialogue between peers and supervisor, communication must be encouraged and supported by commonly held values and standards that it is "okay" to openly communicate and to disagree.[131] Values shape the development and use of technology by the leader (and/or supervisor) to support employees.[132] Whether or not values "take" for any employee is dependent on individual commitment, desire, peer pressures, the environment, and of course the rewards/reinforcements of the company.[133] We will always move in the direction of our number one value and away from what threatens that value.[134]

VALUES AND LEADERSHIP WITHIN ORGANIZATIONS

Kouzes and Posner's (1987) nationwide survey of nearly 1,500 managers reported that the values most frequently sought and admired in their supervisors were integrity (truthfulness, is trustworthy, has character, has convictions); competence (is capable, is productive, is efficient); and leadership (is inspiring, is decisive, provides direction). A follow-up survey also conducted by Kouzes and Posner, sponsored by the federal Executive Institute alumni Association, of nearly 800 senior executives, reported that the values sought and admired were honesty, competence, forward-looking, and inspiring.[135]

The Leadership Voices™: 1995 Washington State Survey obtained strikingly similar results (see Table 1).[136] In this survey the most frequently named core values were integrity, family, God, truth, justice, equality, love, authenticity, duty and loyalty.

Overall, the general consensus is that leaders must be self-aware and be internally consistent in order to develop and sustain authenticity, community, and vision.[137] It is clear that leadership and management skills are not identical and it is not necessarily desirable that they be interchangeable.[138] However, leaders and managers must have common, organizational service or product standards regarding productivity and work principles.[139] In listing the rudimentary elements of self-awareness, a multitude of terms and phrases are used to recognize a leader's core or sacred values, which in turn connote formative social norms and mores.[140]

TYPES OF VALUES

When the word "values" is used as a noun (his values), synonyms include: ideals, standards, morals, principles; customs, institutions, social mores. However, when the word "value" is used as a verb the synonyms are: to prize, to appreciate, to esteem, to admire, to revere, to respect, and to venerate.[141] A leader's incorrect grammatical interpretation of the word "value," filtered through her unique experiential paradigms, can produce substantial undiscovered internal inconsistencies. These internal inconsistencies can produce erroneous self-reflection, internal conflict, disharmony, and disease, which can manifest as:

- an inability to communicate clearly,
- an inability to consciously evolve community,
- an inability to create envisioned form, and
- an inability to distinguish core values from situational conviction.

Inability to distinguish core values from situational conviction(s) is the paradox confronted by many mangers. Managers are required to be timely, responsible, productive, and to meet the "bottom line," while concurrently being expected to be proactive, to empower staff, and to create and sustain a "healthy work environment." Often these differing goals are not compatible. Since managers are responsible for transmitting the leader's voice to employees or followers in order to create the envisioned work environment, efficiency, and proficiency, attention needs to be given to validating transformational "management" and not merely transformational leadership.

Managers are increasingly charged with the responsibility to emulate leadership principles and simultaneously are held accountable to achieve quantifiable productivity. Managers suffer from even greater seemingly innocuous shifts in the grammatical use of the word "value" when social values and traditional (American Christian) work ethics/values are considered. Table 3 presents a sum-

Table 3. Summary of Literature Review Terms and Phrases

Management Values	Leadership Values	Social Values	Traditional Work Values (American Christian)
Effective	Empowering	Determines propensity	Reflection
Efficient	Communicative	Fashions Controls	Community
Profitable	Steward	Authorizes power	Self-discipline
Controlling	Enlightened	Constructs mores	Mentoring
Authoritative	Visionary	Congeals restrictions	Continuous learning
Masterful	Credible	Validates prejudices	Transcendence
Trustworthy	Enlightened	Justifies judgement	Structural hierarchy
Accountable	Conscious	Directs growth	Servant leadership
Responsible	Competent	Creates form	Ethics and principles
Adept	Effective	—	Vocation
—	Mentor	—	Voice creates form

mary of the literature's terms for "value" so that a comparative review may be made of the words ascribed to management values, leadership values, social values and traditional (American Christian) work values. An individual's values, intentions, commitment, and conscious awareness are alive and substance forming with and by their words.

The complexity of clear communication escalates (for both the sender and the recipient) when the manager, who may lack internal congruence regarding his core values, must now transmit the leader's visions and values to his subordinates. Subordinates must then filter the ascribed work values through their personal social norms and mores. Significant problems occur when individuals incorrectly assume the stated value of someone is identical to their own. In fact, the stated value (work efficiency, productivity, teamwork), of one individual is defined by the filters of either: "management values," "leadership values," "social values," or the "traditional American Christian work values" so the definitions of work efficiency, productivity, teamwork differ for each person. The person to whom this value is being sent and/or discussed of course "hears" the valued filtered through his the filter of either "management values," "leadership values," "social values," or the "traditional American Christian work values." The probability for different filters on the value being molded by the manager increases with each employee supervised. Then, when additional perception filters such as age, ethnic and cultural affiliations, and gender are added the chances that two or more individuals realize they are attempting to achieve the same values (vision and voice) exponentially deteriorate. The classic result is low worker moral, performance evaluation disputes, increased misconduct all resulting in the deterioration of the business' products and services.

The leader must take time to discover and explore her personal core values and the core values operative in the work environment. Most importantly, the leader must align her acts and behavior to make sure that they are congruent with, reinforce, and nurture her core values. Then she must support and nurture, the highest values in others. The leader must not confuse goals with values. A goal is an act or concept that is intended to be accomplished; whereas a value is something one believes.[142]

Another management style and value consideration is the manager's gender. Females bring a different set of experiences to the formulation of their value judgments than do men.[143] One of the benefits of Gilligan's research has been the acknowledgment that individuals need to balance personal and professional aspects of their lives. We need to accept "being in balance" as a value. Personal authenticity is another value that has been prioritized by women.

Collectively, we have come to recognize that if a manager communicates from his own values and assumes fair play, there is less tendency to feel frustrated, bitter, angry, and betrayed. Additionally, learning to recognize and support the values of others tends to make both individuals happier, more fulfilled, and committed to friends, employees, associates, and family members. People are motivated by values that may or may not coincide with the leaders' or managers'.

Simply put, a motivational manager is able to balance "managing" to achieve the bottom line with building and sustaining collaborative (team) community values. This manager is able to distinguish the difference between his personal core values and situational convictions. This ability to differentiate is important so that the manager can "walk his talk" with authenticity—and—model appropriate behaviors for subordinates to build and sustain a health work environment. Leaders and business appointing authorities must remember that their voice is "heard" by their followers and employees through the management styles molded by those to whom they have delegated administrative authority. If you are a manager the workforce you have is what you created and sustain. If you have a difficult employee the first place to start "fixing things" is with yourself, once you change so will those over whom you have administrative authority.

TEAMWORK, BUILDING WORK COMMUNITY, SYNCHRONICITY

Only if the future matters can the prospect of doing unto others make a short-term sacrifice seem worthwhile. Caring about the future, however, is not enough. Only if you believe that by supporting the collective interest you will cause others to join you, does the future give you any selfish incentive to do so. And the only way you can assess how much of a difference you can make, and whether it will be enough, is if you pay attention to the actions of others. If it looks like enough people are joining in, you may decide that it is worth joining in also. If not, you won't. As a consequence, the decision of whether or not to cooperate depends critically on what we call coordination externalities.

Duncan J. Watts

A leader is one person who's ability to influence others to act or refrain from acting in the desired way is significantly different from a group of individuals who apparently spontaneously, collectively achieve focused direction and/or purpose. When an individual's self-interest reaches symmetry behaving rationally is self-perpetuating because the individual observes the work environment, relationships, and profitability are enhanced. Another way of saying this is if there is no reward or profitability to being a bully or difficult person an individual will not become one, or will stop their "difficult" behaviors. When co-workers observe or experience the rewards associated with successful teamwork they will voluntarily exhibit the successful modeled behaviors. As each individual worker models the successful behaviors acknowledged in the work unit the synchronicity becomes self-perpetuating if not self-directing. Leaders either develop or emerge because their values and vision are synchronized with the team's spirit.

Leadership by values occurs by the leader first critically examining his own behaviors in relationship to the vales that he professes and then through disciplined awareness achieving internal congruence with his core values. Kreitner and Kinicke's (1992), *Organizational Behavior* stresses throughout their findings that a leader can not say one thing and be another; employees will not put values into practice if the leader does not practice them. The leader's values should influence the character and tone of managers and the company.[144] However, it is not enough just to get leaders (and those to whom

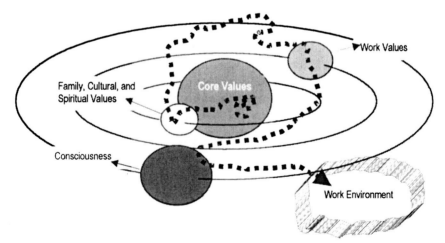

Figure 4.1.   Values Create the Work Environment.

administrative authority and responsibility have been delegated) to "get" and accept the company's values; it is equally important that the entire workforce "get" and accepts these same (work) values.[145]

Training programs and common core curriculum are important ways to communicate values. Because "training" cannot go against an individuals fundamental beliefs leadership programs must allow individuals to reflect on their own values and formulate what they want to get from work.[146]

Robert Hass, Chairman and CEO of Levi Straus and Company, was asked what type of leadership was necessary to make his organization value statement a reality.[147] He responded:

1. New behaviors. Leadership that exemplifies directness and openness to new influences, commitment to the success of others, willingness to acknowledge the leader's own contributions to the problems, personal accountability, teamwork, and trust. We must not only model these behaviors, we must encourage and coach others to adopt them.[148]
2. Diversity. Leadership that values a diverse workforce, including age, sex, and ethnic groups at all levels of the organization. Workforce diversity also includes diversity in perspective and experience. We are committed to taking full advantage of the rich backgrounds and abilities of all of our people and to promoting greater diversity in positions of influence. Different points of view will be valued and honesty rewarded, not suppressed.
3. Recognition. Leadership that provides greater recognition, both financial and physical for individuals (and teams) is contributing to our success. Recognition is to be given to all who contribute, who are creative and innovative, and who continuously support daily operational requirements.
4. Ethical management practices. Leaders must epitomize the standards of ethical behavior. A leader must provide clarity about his expectations and enforce these standards throughout the organization.
5. Communication. Leaders must clearly state goals and performance standards. Employees must know what is expected and be given timely and honest feedback on their performance and career aspirations.
6. Empowerment. Leaders that increase the authority and responsibility for product quality and customer satisfaction are empowering. Responsibility, trust, and recognition should be directed to the outcome, product, or service delivery.[149]

Downsizing and Values

A company's values—what it stands for, what its people believe in—are crucial to its competitive success.[150] Retaining a highly committed workforce with values during downsizing is possible with mutual honesty, commitment, and trust between management and labor. Because employment security cannot be promised, management cannot play games with anyone.[151] It is certainly disingenuous to champion values such as empowerment and commitment when workers are faced with loosing their jobs.

> Sometimes, the only solution is to close the plant and if we don't have the guts to face that decision then we risk hurting a lot of people, not just those in one plant. We need to be honest about this (layoff possibilities) and tie this to our aspirations, mission and vision statement(s) by asking how we are going to treat people who are displaced by technology, changes in production sources or by market changes.
>
> We are committed to making the transition as successful as possible and to minimizing the worker's uprooting and dislocation.
>
> We give more advance notice than is required by law, provide more severance than is typical in our industry so the effect of displacement is cushioned. Additionally, we extend health care benefits, support job training programs and other training initiatives to help our former employees find new jobs.
>
> The community has been depending on us as a major employer. So, we continue to fund, for a period of time, community organizations and social causes we had previously been involved with. So that our withdrawal was not a "double hit" of loss, both of employment and philanthropic support.
>
> Harvard Business Review 1992

However, Hess did acknowledge that being mindful of his personal values and the company's values may slow decisions. Management tends to be more personally challenged, more explicitly examining some factors or giving more weight to some factors than otherwise might have been afforded. The impact of plant closing on the community certainly was one factor that received more consideration. He has at times decided not to close a plant even though the cost to the company would be higher. However, other plants he has closed. The distinguishing factor was the impact on the community.[152] Being constantly aware of one's value hierarchy is empowering, facilitating, and obtaining goals that are congruent with the identified values.[153]

In extreme contrast, Bridges (1994) discusses employment arrangements that are too fluid and idiosyncratic (referred to as "fishnet") to be called a job. Microsoft is given as an example. Microsoft keeps no regular employee hours; the buildings are open to workers twenty-four hours day. Hours worked are not recorded or tracked; only employee output is noted. Employees are not accountable to conventional managers, but to project teams of which they are a part. Each project team is a subset of a larger group, or there may be many projects-within-larger project groupings. Within each team, individual members are always given just a little more than they can personally accomplish, thus necessitating constant collaboration among team members and between teams. Employees move to a new project upon completion of each project. Membership in the next project team is based upon the employee's reputation from previous projects. There are no standardized career routs.[154]

This flattened, quality-driven, fishnet organization lacks the normal job description that sets standards for performing a normal or satisfactory job. Employees here are expected to do anything necessary to accomplish the expected results. The freedom and flexibility found in quality-driven teams typically result in the "normal" and "satisfactory" being converted into synonyms for "substandard." Microsoft employees, like those at many de-jobbed companies, are expected to work beyond the limits that any job could set for them.[155]

Sacred Values and Proactive Management

Mapes (1996) asserts that they are beliefs about what is important, unique to the individual, developed from socialization and personal experience. Values are mental maps of the individual's thoughts concerning the way things should be; representing the individual's deepest convictions, filtering the way reality is viewed. Values are the "hard drive" of the subconscious, a "collective" belief systems defining good and bad, right and wrong. Values are the individual's personal compass, providing a framework for decision-making. Without this framework, self-confidence is lost along with security in making decisions. Values determine one's responses to experiences, how one is satisfied, when one feels happy and fulfilled or violated and empty. If an individual's goals and behavior are incongruent with her values, the result is inner conflict and stress.[156]

For each of us, there is always one value that is most important, one core value driving all the preferences. The benefits of being aware of one's core values include but may not be limited to the following:

1. Determines the individual's perceptions of situations.
2. Determines the individual's decision-making process.
3. Determines the individual's career advancement and success.
4. Determines the individual's standards for ethical behavior.
5. Determines the individual's ability to change and flex amidst chaos.
6. Determines the individual's interpersonal relations.[157]

The term "sacred" traditionally associated with religious philosophies is increasingly being used more in a sociological or in an instrumentally philosophic connotation. When used in this context the term, "sacred" or core values, reference the impregnable and inalterable energy affixed to the value.[158]

Instrumental philosophy asks what is it good for? From an instrumental perspective, a person is not valued because he is a good worker but in terms of his usefulness in meeting someone's needs in some fashion. Sociologically, people and objects are sacred when they are valued for themselves; not for what instrumental use they serve. This definition of sacred is important because Yankelovich's (1981) research suggested that American seekers of self-fulfillment are reassessing what is sacred and what is instrumental in American life. Should people in the workplace be exploited exclusively for instrumental purposes or do they also have intrinsic value.[159]

Discovering one's hierarchy of values is the first step, clarifying the meaning is the second step. This transformation and clarification of values, along with creating a personal vision statement, is not enough to make the quantum leap—one must act.[160] The following five quantum leap values are achievable only after the identification of personal core values:

1. Respect. Having respect for the dignity of the individual is the most import of the five quantum values. Respect governs the way one communicates with, sees, and values people. Respect is the springboard to clarity, compassion, fairness, and service, challenging traditional ways of thinking, awakening one's awareness of interconnectedness, compassion and empathy. Respect for the individual is the antidote to prejudice jealously, envy manipulation and deceit.
2. Accountability. Doing what is felt in the heart to be right, regardless of criticism, opens one to personal freedom, but there are "costs." Being accountable defuses the mythical "they did it" excuse, "they forgot to tell me," "they messed up the works." Freedom of speech accompanied by accountability means each individual takes the role of "player" instead of "victim." In the final analysis, accountability places one's destiny in her own hands.
3. Integrity. Acting with "integrity" goes beyond honesty and sincerity; it means completeness, wholeness or an unimpaired condition, and congruence with what one said and does.
4. Perseverance. Exercising the steadfast tenacity of "perseverance" is irreplaceable, learned and developed.
5. Discipline. Discipline is a verb, an attribute linked to commitment. Discipline and commitment make the difference between resignation and achievement (with or without adversity), settling for mediocrity or striving for excellence.[161] Uncovering and prioritizing "core" values provides the platform for motivation.[162]

While it is inevitable that the selective tradition follows the lines of the growth of the society, it is also a complex, double-edged sword because it is impossible to prejudge the relevance of a past work based on future need. Therefore, even with the natural pressures to follow the growth of the natural society, it is a wise society that, while preserving reflections of current needs and values, society retains values which may appear to be divergent or opposite of current need.

John Storey

SPIRITUAL AND CULTURAL VALUES
AND PROACTIVE MANAGEMENT

Peck (1987)[163] discusses the process of spiritual development, which in many aspects are similar to the four stages of development outlined by Hall and Thompson (1980). Peck's four stages of spiritual development are:

- Phase 1. In the first and primitive stage of group formation, people are frequently pretenders. Pretenses, exhibited in-group formation include the affectation of being loving and pious, covering up the lack of principles. This group tries to look like a community without doing any of the work involved.
- Phase 2. Individuals in this phase have begun the work of submitting themselves to the "principle of the law," but they do not yet understand the "spirit of the law." Consequently, Phase 2 people are legalistic and dogmatic. They are threatened by anyone who thinks differently from them and regard it as their personal responsibility to save those who do not think like them.
- Phase 3. This stage is one of questioning and is analogous to the critical stage of emptiness in community formation. In reaching for community the individuals at this phase must question themselves.
- Phase 4. At this fourth and final phase, individuals within the community must begin to empty themselves of the dogma of skepticism.

Similarly, Hall and Thompson (1980)[164] identified the transformation of an individual through four phases of consciousness in the following ways:

- Phase 1. The world is perceived mysterious and the individual has no control. The individual merely exists in a hostile world. In this phase of consciousness the individual focuses on satisfying basic survival, sensual, and security needs.

- Phase 2. The individual struggles to belong and win approval, acceptance, and success. It is at this phase that the individual becomes aware of "self-worth" and self-esteem. Self-esteem is achieved by meeting the expectations of significant others, first family then peers and finally established institutions. Personal growth is predicated on the affirmation and acceptance of significant others.
- Phase 3. It is within this phase that the individual, for the first time, takes authority seriously and the individual's behavior is characterized by independence, creativity, self-confidence and being self-directed. At this stage, the world is perceived as "created." Here the individual must participate. It is here that the individual begins to prize creativity, imagination, and honesty while finding conformity hypocritical. At this phase the individual begins to actualize his own being, becoming sensitive to the rights of all humans. Liberation, freedom, and independence become matters greater than personal development; they become matters for group social action and national liberation. (It is apparently at this stage of development that Bellah is concerned too many individuals "get stuck").
- Phase 4. At this final phase, the individual self is transcended and the individual acts interdependently with other selves. The "I" transforms to "we." At this phase, like-minded people see the world as a mystery, but a mystery in which men and women must take authority to choose to create and enhance the environment. The mode of transcendence is production and must accomplish new opportunities for the human spirit to emerge. There is a harmonious balance, a feeling of wholeness, and the understanding of interrelatedness. There is an understanding that harmony and balance must be extended to technology as well as society at large.

Simply put, your values determine not only if, but also how you will react to a bully, determinedly difficult person, or predator. Your values determine whether or not your self-worth, your attitude, and your life outside work will be negatively impacted by your nemesis at work. Your values determine whether or not you will pick something equally reprehensible, but different, as an escape from your nemesis. Your values determine and direct your decision making capabilities, defensive strategies, as well as your communication and behavioral objectives if and when you have to negotiate a settlement. Finally, your values determine what lesson(s) you learn from each experience and your ability to cope with and navigate your life.

NOTES

124. Argyle, Michael, *The Social Psychology of Work*, (Penguin Books: Wrights Lane, London, 1974). Bridges, William. Managing Transitions: Making the Most Of Change. (Addison-Wesley: Massachusetts, 1991). Meehan, Mary, et al., The Future Ain't What It Use To Be. (Penguin Putnam Inc.: New York, 1997). Ritzer, George, The Mcdonaldization Of Society. (Pine Forge Press: Thousand Oaks, 2000). Terkel, Studs, Hard Times: An Oral History of the Great Depression. (Pantheon Books: New York, 1986). Terkel, Studs, Coming of Age: The Story of Our Century By Those Who've Lived It. (The New Press: New York, 1995).

125. Jamieson, David, and Julie O'Mara, *Managing Workforce 2000: Gaining the Diversity Advantage*. Forward by Warren Bennis. (Jossey-Bass: San Francisco, 1991), 6.

126. Jamieson and O'Mara, Managing Workforce, 21.

127. Jamieson and O'Mara, Managing Workforce, 22.

128. Bellah, Robert N. et al, *Habits of the Heart: Individualism and Commitment in American Life*. (Harper and Row: New York, 1985), 79–80.

129. Jamieson and O'Mara, Managing Workforce, 181.

130. James, Jennifer, Thinking in the Future Tense: Leadership Skills for a New Age. (Simon and Schuster: New York, 1996).

131. Compilation (A Harvard Business Review Book), 41–42.

132. Compilation (A Harvard Business Review Book), 39.

133. Compilation (A Harvard Business Review Book), 47.

134. Mapes, James. J., *Quantum Leap Thinking: An Owner's Guide to the Mind*. (Dove Books: Beverly Hills, 1996), 56.

135. Kouzes James. M. and Barry Z. Posner, *The Leadership Challenge: How To Get Extraordinary Things Done in Organizations*. (San Francisco: Jossey-Bass, 1987), 16.

136. Irby, Linda, Leadership Voices™: Values, Proactive Management, and Consciousness. (*UMI: 304 1369*, 2002).

137. Burns, James M, *Leadership*. (Harper and Row: New York, 1978). Hollander, Edwin. P., *Leadership Dynamics: A Practical Guide to Effective Relationships*. (The Free Press: New York, 1978). Hall Brian P. and Helen Thompson, *Leadership Through Values*, (Paulist Press: New York, 1980). Kouzes James. M. and Barry Z. Posner, *The Leadership Challenge: How To Get Extraordinary Things Done in Organizations*. (San Francisco: Jossey-Bass, 1987). Locke, Ewin A., et al., *The Essence of Leadership: The Four Keys to Leading Successfully*. (Lexington Books: New York, 1991). Terry, Robert. W., *Authentic Leadership: Courage in Action*. (Jossey-Bass: San Francisco,1993).

138. Bass, Bernard M., Bass and Stogdill's Handbook of Leadership: Theory, Research and Managerial Applications. (The Free Press: New York, 1990). Bennis, Warren and Burt Nanus. (1985). Leaders: The Strategies for Taking Charge. Harper and Row: New York. Wall et al., , The Visionary Leader: From Mission Statement to A Thriving Organization, Here's Your Blueprint for Building an Inspired Cohesive, Customer-Oriented Team. (Prima: Rocklin, Cal.,1992), Walton, Clarence C., The Moral Manager. (Harper Business: New York, 1988). Yukl, Gary. A., Leadership in Organizations. (Prentice Hall: Enlewood Cliffs, N.J., 1981).

139. Bass, Bernard M., *Bass and Stogdill's Handbook of Leadership: Theory, Research and Managerial Applications*. (The Free Press: New York, 1990). Gretz, Karl. F. and Steven R. Drozdeck, *Empowering Innovative People*. (Prous Publishing Company: Chicago, 1992). Moss, Leonard, *Management Stress*. (Addison-Wesley Publishing Co., 1981). Rosen, Robert, *Healthy Companies: A Human Resource Approach (AMA Management Briefing)*. (AMA Membership Publications Division, AMA, NY, 1986). Rosen, Robert with Lisa Berger, *The Healthy Company: Eight Strategies to Develop People, Productivity and Profits*. (Jeremy P. Tarcher/Perigree: New York, 1991). Weisbord, Marvin R., *Productive Workplaces: Organizing and Managing for Dignity, Meaning, and Community*. (Jossey-Bass: San Francisco, 1987).

140. Bellah, Robert N. et al, *Habits of the Heart: Individualism and Commitment in American Life*. (Harper and Row: New York, 1985). Burns, James M, *Leadership*. (Harper and Row: New York, 1978). Hall Brian P. and Helen Thompson, *Leadership Through Values*, (Paulist Press: New York, 1980). Hammond Joshua and James Morrison, *Stuff Americans Are Made Of: Seven Cultural Forces That Define Americans— A New Framework For Quality, Productivity And Profitability*. (Simon and Schuster Macmillan Company: New York, 1996). Hollander, Edwin. P., *Leadership Dynamics: A Practical Guide to Effective Relationships*. (The Free Press: New York, 1978). Kouzes James. M. and Barry Z. Posner, *The Leadership Challenge: How To Get Extraordinary Things Done in Organizations*. (San Francisco: Jossey-Bass, 1987). Locke, Ewin A., et al., *The Essence of Leadership: The Four Keys to Leading Successfully*. (Lexington Books: New York, 1991). Terry, Robert. W., *Authentic Leadership: Courage in Action*. (Jossey-Bass: San Francisco,1993).

141. Burns, James M, *Leadership*. (Harper and Row: New York, 1978). Hall Brian P. and Helen Thompson, *Leadership Through Values*, (Paulist Press: New York, 1980). Locke, Ewin A., et al., *The Essence of Leadership: The Four Keys to Leading Successfully*. (Lexington Books: New York, 1991). Terry, Robert. W., *Authentic Leadership: Courage in Action*. (Jossey-Bass: San Francisco,1993).

142. Rodale, Jerome I., *The Synonym Finder: Special Deluxe Edition*.(Rodale Press: Emmaus, Pa., 1978).

143. Mapes, *Quantum Leap*, 109.

144. Gilligan, Carol, In A Different Voice: Psychological Theory and Women's Development. (Harvard University Press: Cambridge, 1993).

145. Compilation (Harvard Business Review), 46.

146. Compilation (Harvard Business Review), 49.

147. Compilation (Harvard Business Review), 45.

148. Compilation (Harvard Business Review), 51.

149. Compilation (Harvard Business Review), 53.

150. Compilation (Harvard Business Review), 51.

151. Compilation (Harvard Business Review), 35.

152. Compilation (Harvard Business Review), 50.

153. Compilation (Harvard Business Review), 51.

154. Mapes, *Quantum Leap*, 111.

155. Bridges, William. *Managing Transitions: Making the Most Of Change*. (Addison-Wesley: Massachusetts, 1991), 41.

156. Bridges, Managing Transitions, 41.

157. Mapes, *Quantum Leap*, 107.

158. Mapes, James. J., *Quantum Leap Thinking: An Owner's Guide to the Mind.* Dove Books: Beverly Hills, 1996). Hitt, William D., *Ethics and Leadership: Putting Theory into Practice.* (Battelle Press: Columbus, Ohio, 1990).

159. English Harace B, and Ava C. English, A Comprehensive Dictionary of Psychological And Psychoanalytical Terms. A Guide to Usage, for Readers and Writers in the Fields of Psychology, Psychoanalysis, Psychiatry, Education, Guidance, and Social Work. (David McKay Company, Inc.: New York, 1966). Rodale, Jerome I., The Synonym Finder: Special Deluxe Edition. (Rodale Press: Emmaus, Pa., 1978).

160. Yankelovich, Daniel, New Rules: Searching for Self-Fulfillment in a World Turned Upside Down. (Random House: New York, 1981), 7.

161. Mapes, *Quantum Leap*, 113.

162. Mapes, *Quantum Leap*, 116–120.

163. Mapes, *Quantum Leap*, 108.

164. Mapes, *Quantum Leap*, 200–208.

Chapter Five

Christian Tenets and
The American Work Ethic

Although the intellect is easily fooled, the heart recognizes the truth. Where the intellect is limited, the heart is unlimited; where the intellect is intrigued by the temporary, the heart is only concerned with the permanent.

David Hawkins

In order for us to see the possible futures available to us as American employers, employees, consumers, and international traders, we must understand who we are today is directly induced by our traditional work ethic. Comprehending that American culture is inextricably interwoven into American business methods, means and kinds of work is compelling since American traditional work ethics has it's roots in the Christian work ethic. Comprehending American culture provides the basis for a new understanding of why some "best business practices" today work or fail to meet our expectations.

Transformational leaders and proactive managers envision and create new opportunities and quite often challenge old assumptions: sometimes intentionally, sometimes not. Successful leaders and managers appreciate that at any one time we always have several generations in our work force: some born and raised in America, some not. The friction in today's American business ethics regarding leadership, management, and profitability is the interface between the "traditional American work ethic" and the new paradigms of commerce in today's global economy. And as Americans, collectively whether we like it or not, we each have a history and we are each in some way intertwined in a global economy that demands from us (individually and collectively) alertness, flexibility, quicker responses, innovation, and creativity.[165]

Hammond and Morrison (1996) point out the following characteristics about today's American workforce that must be kept in mind as we review the roots of our " traditional American work ethic:"

- "Americans seem to deny the existence of a collective culture. It is essential for us to see ourselves as individuals, not necessarily as a group, except when push comes to shove. Americans are eager to make a difference. Choice is the dominant force in America.
- The genius of Americans is their ability to turn their personal, corporate, and national dreams, the seemingly impossible, into the possible. Technology is the great enabler, but the dreams must come first.
- Americans are obsessed with "big" and "more." Americans are obsessed with being "number one."
- Americans are impatient, time-obsessed, and believe that time is money. We want what we want and we want it now.
- Americans see making mistakes as a part of how we learn. We unconsciously do not do things right the first time because we are not motivated by a desire for perfection. We learn from our mistakes and this learning has a huge emotional pay-off for us.
- Americans value fixing things more than doing things right the first time. This enables us to show how human we are and how good we can be. The way we fix things—and create breakthroughs—is through improvising. Once the situation is fixed (or almost fixed) we are free to move on to something else, and moving on is a major preoccupation for us.
- Americans have a fixation with "what's new." We are in a perpetual search for new identities, new ideas, new strategies, and new products, because they provide new choices.[166]

Simply put, everyone who works in America is not necessarily born and raised in America and each person's cultural work ethics are different and experienced differently. These cultural work ethics are ingrained in each of us during our formative years and often become part of our core work ethic. Additionally, everyone working in America is not Christian and even if they were there is a reasonable chance that their Christian values are based on different Christian denomination tenets. These two highly variable values constructs (differing cultural work ethics and differing religious core values) coupled with individual emotional and motivational responses to money, power, and vanity provide the ingredients for the "difficult person" and your perception of the difficult person.

CHOICE, DISCIPLINE, PERFORMANCE, PROFIT

It is clear that power is associated with that which supports life, and force is associated with that which exploits life for the gain of an individual or an organization. Force is divisive and, through that divisiveness, weakens, whereas power unifies. Force polarizes. . . . Force is seductive because it emanates certain glamour . . . The weak are attracted to, and will even die for the glamour of force.

David R. Hawinks

Construction of a convincing review of leadership and management history in relation to traditional American businesses and organizations necessarily abuts Christian tenets.[167] The scope of this literature review will be limited to select works discussing Christian tenets only in relationship to traditional American work ethics. The developing spectrum of popular awareness is recognizing that one's religious and spiritual values do have an influencing and motivational affect on one's business leadership, management, and profits. Two contemporary, influential researchers in this field are Dr. M. Scot Peck and the research team Dr. Brian P. Hall and Dr. Helen Thompson. Dr. Peck, a psychiatrist, focuses on the need for individuals to confront and resolve problems, emphasizing that individuals suffering through changes can ultimately reach a higher level of self-understanding. The team of Dr. Hall and Dr. Thompson focused their research on work, values, and value consciousness development.

For Peck, Hall, and Thompson, the bully, determinedly difficult person, or predator reside in the first stage or phase of conscious awareness. These difficult individuals are consumed with primary survival motivations, focused on self-gratification, and often incapable of respecting the boundaries of "others." By the time this individuals begins to self-actualize, question the significance of others basic needs they are entering stage or phase 2 of their conscious development. A comparison and contrasting of these contemporary works, in Table 4, shows that as the conscious awareness of the individual increases so to does the individual's ability to perceive interconnectivity and focus on manifesting one's visions.

Bullies, determinedly difficult people, and predators have many characteristics the most damaging to you at work is they are without scruples, driven by fear and simultaneously compelled to deny this same motivational fear. Their insecurities can be injurious to you, limit your choices and freedom, and through repeated and sustained contact with these abusers distort your sense of self-worth and over time lower your conscious awareness. The proliferation of bullies, determinedly difficult people, and predators at work has contributed to the shift in work expectations identified in Yankelovich's 1981, research.

Table 4.   Comparison of Peck's Process of Spiritual Awareness to Hall and Thompson's Phases of Development

Peck's Process of Spiritual Awareness	Hall and Thompson's Phases of Development	Hall and Thompson's Core Values
Stage 1: People are frequent Pretenders.	Phase 1: The world is a mystery.	Phase 1: Self-preservation.
Stage 2: People have submitted to the principles of laws.	Phase 2: The world is social.	Phase 2: Belonging, self-worth and self-confidence.
Stage 3: People start questioning, the beginning of awareness.	Phase 3: The world is a project.	Phase 3: Self-actualization, service, human dignity, intimacy, and solitude.
Stage 4: People begin to release skepticism.	Phase 4: The world is a mystery to be cared for.	Phase 4: Interdependence.

Yankelovich's (1981) research revealed several American consciousness states that are undergoing shifts: the shift from economic optimism to gloom; the shift from trust in institutions to mistrust, and finally the shift from confidence in American's future to a jumpy apprehensiveness. These shifts in American consciousness, apparent from Yankelovich's research, indicate a hopeful and inwardly focused America, aware of opportunity for self-expression. If there have been shifts in consciousness, then these shifts have occurred as the adherence to Christian tenets or the traditional American "values" and "work ethics" have shifted.

HISTORICAL SYNOPSIS OF CHRISTIANITY

According to the 1993 Parliament of Religions held in Chicago, demographers estimate that there will be approximately somewhere around one billion Christians as the twentieth century unfolds. So, numerically speaking, Christianity is the largest religion in the world. Of this number, slightly more than half of all Christians are Roman Catholics, the remainder of this number is comprised of Protestants, Orthodox Christians (found mainly in Greece, Russia and Eastern Europe) and various branches of Pentecostalism, which is apparently the fastest-growing Christian movement anywhere in the world today. In America alone there are nearly five hundred separate and distinct forms of Christianity. With this range in Christian practices, it is difficult to generalize about Christianity. In some instances there are dramatic differences regarding "who" Jesus Christ was/is; however, all Christians tend to agree that Jesus Christ is pivotal and indispensable to Christianity.

Jesus Christ lived for approximately 33 years in a remote outpost of the Roman Empire nearly 2,000 ago. If the question is asked, who is Jesus Christ, different answers must be expected because only part of the response can come from history, another part from a denomination's tenets, and the rest of the response (for the Christian) comes form the heart.

The 1993 Parliament of Religions-Chicago pointed out that there are three irreducible elements common to all who "reasonably" call themselves Christian, even though these three components assume diverse forms and carry different weights in the lives of Christians. The first of these common elements are the core ideas of Christianity, second are all part of the Christian community, and finally each has a relationship (however mediated or indirect) to the person of Jesus Christ.

Christian sacraments (sometimes called ordinances suggesting these actions be specifically ordered by Jesus Christ himself) supply the symbolic nourishment for Christian tenets. The 1993 Parliament of Religions-Chicago, defined "sacrament" as the outward and visible sign of an inward and invisible reality. While Christians differ among and between themselves regarding the number of sacraments or ordinances, Christians tend to practice some form of observance of the following:

1. Baptism, symbolizing the entrance into the community of the church.
2. Communion, sometimes referred to as the Eucharist or the Lord's Supper. This observance tends to be among the most controversial, even though almost all Christians participate in this observance in some form.
3. Marriage is included as a sacrament in some churches. Because marriages tend to be one of the few times people in a religiously pluralistic society have an opportunity to observe another's traditions' this tenet is somewhat familiar to almost everyone.
4. Ordination is important in those Christian churches that have ordained clergy. Various churches have their different ways of ascertaining whether or not an individual has received a genuine call, but it is typically agreed that neither personal talents, tastes or education suffice to make a persona eligible for ordination: a "call" is essential.[168]
5. Confession, sometimes known as the sacraments of Penance or Reconciliation, is practiced in a variety of ways in different churches, but its inner meaning is similar.
6. Finally, for some Christians, there is a sacrament sometimes called "Extreme Unction," where the person is anointed with oils accompanied with special prayers.

In sum, these various Christian sacraments, regardless of how many or the method of observance, acknowledge that God has a purpose for them as people in the world.

Right about now you may be asking what has this historical review of traditional American work ethics, firmly rooted in Christianity, got to do with me and my nemesis? Answer, if you, some of your family and friends were born and/or raised in America you have some basic assumptions about "fair play", a good supervisor, and your work "rights." When someone violates your "rights" and/or your sense of "fair play" at work you then start to look for the "laws" that protect you. Laws, work policies, and contract language are only beginning to protect workers against the verbal abuse and sometimes-physical intimidation of bullies, determinedly difficult people, and predators at work. If you were not born and/or raised in America, then you may be trying to figure out all the "unwritten" rules at work. But what typically tends to happen is you just tend to keep your mouth shut, shake your head to yourself and most probably think, "Americans are crazy."

People being plagued by one or more nemesis at work is not new. However, the increasing recognition of the bully's damage to their prey, and the prohibition of the bully's disruptive and abusive behavior's is a shift in best business practice. The question then becomes since there is a link between traditional American work ethics and Christianity, is a new type of Christianity evolving?[169] If so, is this apparent evolution of Christian tents the catalyst or casualty of the change in American values that is affecting all aspects of today's business communities? This review of the literature only focuses on "traditional" Christian tenets shaping "traditional" American work ethics.

John Calvin and the American Work Ethic

Ethics and leadership go hand-in-hand. An ethical environment is conducive to effective leadership, and effective leadership is conducive to ethics. Effective leadership is a consequence of ethical leadership. Ethics and leadership function as both cause and effect.

William D. Hitt

John Calvin (1509 to 1564), was a French reformer and theologian. According to Livingstone (1977), Calvinism is the theological system derived from Calvin's postulations and are in substantial agreement with Lutheran beliefs: the Bible is the only rule of faith, there is denial of human free will after the Fall of Adam, and the doctrine of justification by faith alone. However, Calvinism added the doctrines of the inadmissibility of grace and the gratuitous predestination of some to salvation and others to damnation.[170] These tenets, when applied in a capitalist society and workplace, contribute to the capitalist tendency to expect individuals to choose their provision, working loyally and diligently on the one hand; while on the other hand imposing total responsibility on the individual for failure, expunging all employer accountability.

The overall impact of Calvinism resulted in the following core values relating to the American Work Ethic, as we know it:

1. The improvement of society and government depended on the improvement of human beings. Therefore, a critical arena for reformation was the church, for in his opinion, only through the grace of the Holy Spirit could the human heart reform.[171]
2. Utilitarianism, another essential value, for which Calvin regularly evaluated human society for its utility. This same principle, however, gave Calvin's social ethic a degree of flexibility. For example, he contended that one should act "rightly" for one's-self but not put pressure on others to follow their example as if it were a rule.
3. Calvin also thought private property was fundamental to social order. Calvin believed that each person should possess what is his own; that acquisition of property might vary, but each person should increase her means by ingenuity, physical strength or any other means. In short, Calvin equated political order with each individual "holding" her own.[172]

Take a moment to reflect. Does this "work ethic" resemble any management philosophy where you work? This particular work ethic, while having much merit also has the necessary ingredients required to cultivate and sustain bullies, determinedly difficult people, and predators. Ever wonder why senior executives and administrators know the bullies and predators (many of them managers and supervisors) behaviors toward individuals in the workforce, yet nothing is ever done to change or stop the offensive practices. Well, senior executives and administrators subscribe to the Calvinist's conflicting ideas of expecting that individuals should act right but not pressure others to follow their example, while simultaneously holding that the individual is totally responsible for her failures, then the burden of "getting along" is transferred to you. Meanwhile, you and the bully are expected to "hold your own" and advance by ingenuity, physical strength or any other means. Thus you the prey not the disruptive, abusive, predator, are responsible for your circumstances.

Max Weber and the American Work Ethic

Max Weber (1504 to 1558), was a social and theological researcher and analyzer. His analysis of Christian (and particularly Protestant) tenets are given significant recognition for forming the core of the "Protestant Ethic," or work ethic in the sixteenth century. This work ethic enabled the emerging merchant class to accumulate wealth, keep profits, claim extensive personal freedom, and is the primary basis for capitalism. The core values established by Weber are:

1. Work as a calling. Unlike other societies that traditionally regarded work as a means of survival, the equation of work to a calling provided significant motivation for production of more than is necessary for survival.
2. Success as a sign of grace. Success in one's occupation was a clear sign of divine favor, therefore provided motivation for "hard work."
3. Individuals as monitors of their own state of grace. The individual alone is responsible for his or her own fate. As with Calvin, this philosophy diminished or released employers from obligations to employees.

Weber separated capitalistic enterprise from the pursuit of gain. He contended that the desire for wealth had existed in many places, throughout out time, and thus as such had nothing to do with capitalistic action. Weber contended that capitalism was found primarily in the West and in relatively recent times, and is associated with rational organization of formally free labor. Rational organization of labor was defined as routinized, calculated administration within continuously functioning enterprises. A rationalized capitalistic enterprise implied two things: a disciplined labor force and the regularized investment of capital.[173]

Weber postulated that the drive to accumulate wealth, associated with Puritanism, is due to the concept of the "calling." The concept of the "calling," according to Weber, did not exist either in antiquity or in Catholic theology; the Reformation introduced it. The meaning of the "calling" is an individual is to perform his personal duty in worldly affairs. The "calling," then projects religious behavior into the day-to-day world, and stands in direct contrast to a (Catholic ideal according to Weber) monastic life. The monastic life's object was to transcend the demands of mundane existence.[174]

Weber asserts the idea of the calling was present in Luther's doctrines, and was rigorously developed by the various Puritan sects: Calvinism, Methodism, Pietism and Baptism. Weber concentrated particular emphasis on Calvinism's doctrine of predestination; only some human beings are saved from damnation, the choice being predetermined by God. Weber maintained that the doctrine of predestination had but one consequence for those who subscribed to it, a feeling of unprecedented inner loneliness. From this misery, Weber maintained the capitalist spirit was born.[175] Ford (1991) on the other hand, states that a "calling" is the acceptance of a moral imperative, "Jesus showed that a true leader does not resist the "must" that God lays on him, and in accepting these moral imperatives they are transformed into a material victory."[176] Individuals "must" not resist the calling because it is a discipleship. True leadership means receiving power from God, and its use is to serve people in God's way. God rules, not leaders. People matter most, not techniques. The heart of leadership is not in mastering the "how-to-do's," but in "being mastered" by the amazing grace of God.[177] Weber maintains that the dynamics of Puritanism had a direct and immediate impact in forming the moral outlook affecting the lower and middle "working classes" by establishing the "virtues" of the "faithful" employee.[178]

Weber's Critics

It is important to put Weber's beliefs in perspective, for many of his proposals were controversial. Weber's research of Protestant ethics was only one of his many studies of world religions that included Judaism, Hinduism, Buddhism, and Confucianism. Also, Weber's analysis of Protestant ethics (as were his other religious analysis), were intended to be part of a study of divergent models of rationalism in culture. This study of rationalism in culture attempted to pursue the significance, if any, of any divergences in socio-economic development. As part of his world religion study, Weber contended that Puritanism was only one element affecting modern capitalism.[179]

Weber's book *The Protestant Ethic*, sparked considerable controversy from contemporary Marxists, for arguing that some religious concepts could have transformative force. Weber described Catholicism as a mundane discipline, which retarded modern economic development and Protestantism as a Puritan sect constraining workers with the doctrine of "calling."[180] The primary critics of Weber's characterization of Protestantism fall into the following categories.

1. Weber was mistaken in presuming Luther introduced the concept of "calling" and that Calvinist ethics were anti-capitalistic.
2. Weber's explanation of Benjamin Franklin's ideas as well as his analysis of American Puritanism are unacceptable.
3. Weber misinterpreted Catholic doctrine.
4. Weber's statement of connections between Puritanism and modern capitalism is based on unsatisfactory empirical evidence.
5. Weber is not justified in drawing as sharp a contrast as he does between modern and rational capitalism.[181]

Initially, Max Weber thought that the Protestant creed produced motivations that were conducive to pro-capitalistic activities. Weber felt that Protestantism of varying degrees, in various denominations and sects had a strong influence in mobilizing the capitalistic ethos.[182]

However, in Weber's later works, he introduced several corrections to his original ideas. He later determined that Protestantism was a contributing factor to capitalism, not the ultimate reason supporting capitalism. Capitalism was a mass motivation for worldly activity.[183]

Take a moment to reflect. Does this "work ethic" resemble any management philosophy where you work? This particular work ethic, while having much merit also has the necessary ingredients required to cultivate and sustain bullies, determinedly difficult people, and predators. As with Calvin, Weber argues that the individual alone is responsible for her fate, then expands this thought to say one's work should be her calling and success the ultimate conclusion. Webber's sanctioning capitalism as in support of "one's calling", rewards bullies and predator's behaviors for they "discipline" the labor force with the result being a loyal and dependable (if not trustworthy) employee.

Everett Hagen

Everett Hagen (circa 1962) introduced to the "discussion" of work ethics the "innovational personality." This personality, according to Hagen, is a prerequisite for economic growth and the spread of capital formation.[184]

Hagen contrasted and compared what he called authoritarian personalities to what he called innovational personalities. His comparisons are summarized in Table 5: Hagen's Innovative Personality and Work Ethics. Some personality traits Hagen considered to be attitudes about reality, the individual's role in the world, styles of leadership, and levels of creativeness and innovation.[185]

Sztompka[186] points out that like Weber, Hagen had to face questions about how the modern innovative personality appears. Weber answered this question stating it was due to the Protestant or Calvinistic religion. However, Hagen concluded this shift occurs when established, predetermined, ascriptive norms are undermined by social mobility. These occurrences resulted in the stratification of hierarchies and the determination of the following "norms."

1. When a group/individual or occupational category loses its status, a gap appears between the group/individuals' or occupational category's earlier and later status.
2. A group or occupational category does not receive the regard its members believe they deserve. The individuals feel that the other groups unjustifiably underestimate their groups. A gap appears between the self-definition of status and the status actually enjoyed.
3. There is a discrepancy or inconsistency between various dimensions of status or prestige. In other words, when the prestige of a certain job does not match the level of income, power, or when a great power or income

Table 5.   Hagen's Innovative Personality and Work Ethics

Characteristic	Authoritarian	Innovational
• Attitudes to reality. • Perception of individual role in the world. • Style of leadership. • Level of creativeness and innovation.	• Compliance to patterns of life dictated by traditions and authority and legitimated by their support of "eternal nature" and supernatural origins. • Submissiveness, obedience, conformity, avoidance of responsibility and a need for dependence. • Rigidity, high expectations, and strict demands directed to subordinates. • Lack of creativeness and innovation.	• Inquisitiveness and manipulative attitude to the world in persistent search for its underlying regularities in order to influence the control of of phenomena. • Taking personal responsibility for the "gad" side of the world coupled with the search for better solutions in an an attempt to introduce change. Openness and tolerance to subordinates, encouraging their originality and innovation. • Putting premium on originality, novelty, and restless curiosity.

does not go together with the level of prestige. This gap appears between the status, a person or occupation receives on the one scale of stratification and the status measured by the "other" scale.

4. When the group is not yet "accepted" in a wider social setting and its members share in its marginal status. The gap appears between a status aspired to and the one actually obtained.

In all four situations, the common denominator is the gap between actual and imagined status. When this gap occurs, the structural inconsistency is manifested by the withdrawal of status. Status withdrawal brings about a certain type of adaptation; this adaptation tends to go from resignation, through ritualistic assurance, through perceived patterns, to innovation and rebellion against the situation perceived as unacceptable. Each of these adaptations occurred under certain specific concrete conditions. For Hagen, innovation and rebellion were the most interesting because to him this explained the emergence of the innovational personality.[187]

Take a moment to reflect. Does this "work ethic" resemble any management philosophy where you work? This particular work ethic, while having much merit also has the necessary ingredients required to cultivate and sustain bullies, determinedly difficult people, and predators. Low self-esteem, loss of self-esteem, and fear for one's self-preservation are intrinsically interwoven when there is "structural inconsistency" and the individual perceives they have no status or their status is in jeopardy. In today's chaotic, changing world this theory supports the general feeling that there are more difficult people than ever at work.

> Only if the future matters can the prospect of doing unto others make a short-term sacrifice seem worthwhile. Caring about the future, however, is not enough. Only if you believe that by supporting the collective interest you will cause others to join you, does the future give you any selfish incentive to do so. And the only way you can assess how much of a difference you can make, and whether it will be enough, is if you pay attention to the actions of others. If it looks like enough people are joining in, you may decide that it is worth joining in also. If not, you won't.
>
> Duncan J. Watts

AMERICAN CLASS, VALUES, AND ETHOS

A collective people's culture usually exhibits more continuity than change, and ordinarily these cultural patterns persist for long periods of time. An analysis of the observed culture's continuity rests on whether or not the subtle changes are noticed, and how and what these subtle changes alter. Yankelovich's research determined important changes are occurring in America which mark a decisive break with the past. The "new rules," achieving personal desire, are establishing a new ethical norm.[188] The following new norms are evolving as American's break with tradition:

1. The preoccupation with self-fulfillment.
2. The individual pursuit to "get ahead."
3. The need for "institutions" to provide both "support" and autonomy.
4. The economy functions more or less automatically.
5. The individuals need to evolve toward commitment.
6. The evolving concept of duty to self pursued at the cost of moral obligation to others.

Yankelovich cites the rapid changes in the nation's economy as one of the most confusing changes. The importance in economic shifts is underscored because there is a disparity between traditional cultural norms and the economy's ability to support these norms. The result, the economy is increasingly less able to reward hard work and sacrifice for the family through "pay." When the cultural "reward" is consistent with the economy, individuals feel a "moral rightness" for hard work and sacrifice for the family. However, current changes in the economy means that the subtle shifts in values are rapidity intensifying. Thus, the ramification of a once subtle shift in economics and values has increased the "feeling" that, either there are no rules or, observing the rules makes no sense. The formation of the "new norms" has tended to make individual feel that compliance with "the (traditional) rules" leaves them empty-handed, while those who flaunt the (traditional) rules are rewarded. Americans are increasingly individually and collectively, suffering extreme and profound demoralization in daily life.[189]

As already seen, traditionally the notion of success as a virtue went along with the belief that success was primarily due to one's own efforts. One's profits from success either needs to be saved, as a precondition for the accumulation of capital which is required to begin a new business, or, spent to support capitalism.

In the last several years there has been resurgence in "traditional" Christian values, "traditional family values" and "ethics in business" by Middle America. The term Middle America is primarily an economic concept, coined by columnist Joseph Kraft in an article published on June 23, 1986. The article focused on the group of Americans (determined by U.S. Labor Department statistics for the year 1967) whose annual earnings fell between $7,000 to $10,000. This article showed that these individuals had requirements that were outrunning their earnings. This article also indicated that there was a conflict between the middle class and the classes above and below—thus the term "middle."[190]

It is Clarence Walton's (1988) assessment that the nation's current reassertion of "dependence" on God occurs when the national experience of the majority of Americans is one of a widespread loss of confidence.[191] Christianity, America's predominant religion has influenced America's colonial culture and is still most-prevalently displayed in: the American work ethic, the role of the family, the moral implications of economic competition, the shape of foreign policy, the right to life and the individual's freedom of choice.[192] Christianity has influenced the traditional American work ethic by:

- providing a framework with which individuals can understand and interpret their own experiences with community;
- emphasizing personal freedoms;
- reducing the national tendency to exhibit inherent moral superiority over others; and
- families, churches and communities have increasingly transferred the function of socializing to an ever expanding and encompassing educational structure.

This significant transference of socialization of youth to an institution, albeit it is an educational system for children, has resulted in individuals feeling free of allegiances to what once were basic institutions: the family, the church and the community. The "unattached" individuals, who are also extremely mobile, tend to act as if they were morally interchangeable parts within our technological society.

A MATTER OF CLASS

According to Hess et al. (1988), Americans are very much aware of class differences, despite their apparent tendency to think of themselves as "middle class." The apparent ability of Americans to sustain the myth of a classless America is primarily due to the lack of class-consciousness. Awareness of class-consciousness occurs when class becomes the central organizing point of self-definition and political actions. In the past there had been no political parties based on class distinctions. However, recently there have been an increasing number of "fraction political parties" with a growing number of American's beginning to listen to their platforms challenging both the Democratic and Republican parties.

Also traditionally, the unequal distribution of resources was tolerated because of the perception of "fairness" of equality. Or put another way, some citizens thought the rules were fair and equal for all; the exceptions being "minorities" who had no political influence to change the "system." Now, along with other cultural "shifts," those individuals who were traditionally considered "minorities" are rapidly becoming the numerical majority. For individuals considered to be "minorities", the rules, and values may not appear to be changing, or if seen to be changing, the change is to afford inclusion, and therefore not changing fast enough.

The perceptions of those adhering to the "traditional values" of equality and fairness have been sustained by the following five ideologies:[193]

1. The promise of equal opportunity. The belief that with hard work and a bit of luck, anyone can rise from "rags to riches."
2. Survival of the fittest. The belief that the naturally superior will win out in the struggle for survival.
3. Psychological determinism. Americans prefer to believe that individual psychological traits, motivation, achievement needs intelligence and so forth, are responsible for success or failure in the workplace.
4. The American work ethic. The American value system is built around the idea that work is a sacred task and that success in one's work can be seen

as a sign of divine grace. Failure, therefore, can signify only a lack of good qualities, because only some moral flaw would account for an inability to hold a job or save money. A moral flaw would include laziness, lack of ambition or absence of self-control.

5. The "culture of poverty." The transmission of values and behaviors, one generation to another, creates a distinct subculture reinforcing the poverty cycle. This transfers the "blame" of poverty to the family, rather than the individual.

A MATTER OF VALUES, AND ETHOS

The distinction between class ethos and values are often overlooked. Class distinctions are learned rules of behavior and are part of social norms. Social norms may be either prescribed (which are definitions of the acceptable), or proscribed (which are definitions of acts that are not acceptable). Values, on the other hand are the central beliefs of a culture that provide the standards by which norms are judged.[194] For example, a set of core values were identified in 1970 by Robin Williams which he called the "American Ethos," that are quite similar to Max Weber's Protestant Ethics.[195] Williams stated ethos were the underlying beliefs and behaviors of Americans that represented to them their conception of the good life and the goals of social action. Williams identified American ethos as:

1. Achievement and success are major personal goals.
2. Activity and work are favored above leisure and laziness.
3. Moral orientation, one's absolute judgments of good and bad, right and wrong.
4. Humanitarian motives shown in acts as supporting charities and crisis aid.
5. Efficiency and practicality, are the preference for the quickest and shortest way to achieve a goal at the least cost.
6. Process and progress, a belief that technology can solve all problems and the future will be better than the past.
7. Material comfort as the American Dream.
8. Equality as an abstract ideal.
9. Freedom as a person's right against the state.
10. External conformity, the ideal of going along, joining, and not rocking the boat.
11. Science and rationality as the means of mastering the environment and securing more material comforts.
12. Nationalism, a belief that American values and institutions represent best on earth.

13. Democracy based on personal equality and freedom.
14. Individualism manifested in emphasis on personal rights and responsibilities.
15. Racism and group-superiority themes, periodically leading to prejudice and discrimination against those who are racially, religiously, and culturally different from white northern Europeans.[196]

An interesting leadership paradox appears to be developing. The American work ethic is changing (tending toward a diminishing devotion to work and an increasing demand for personal fulfillment, family involvement, and enjoyment of the good life). Greater numbers of individuals, who were formerly excluded from meaningful work or decision-making positions, are entering the work environment. At the same time, businesses and organizations are streamlining employment opportunities, and high wages are loosing false support. The simultaneous occurrence of a "backlash" against traditional work values and fewer and less-lucrative job opportunities may not be coincidental. Increasingly Americans are openly questioning whether or not a "backlash" against traditional values is occurring. As American's (personal and collective) awareness of consciousness expands they beginning to question whether their leaders have core values. Will this trend toward wanting, needing to know a leader's core value(s) continue? Will future leaders be able to lead the future workforce, or will there be too great a divergence in worker's "needs" and leader's visions?

AMERICAN WORK VALUES AND BUSINESS ETHICS

The American Dream's "skeletal system," according to Safire, is the American private enterprise system. The American dream's stressing opportunity is considered the force behind government's philosophy; a combination of freedom, opportunity, social justice and the promise of economic freedom to provide a continuously rising standard of life. The term, "American Dream," infers the indistinguishability of private enterprise and economic democracy. Just as the free enterprise system is the skeletal system of the American Dream, so the leader of the business or organization is the skeletal system creating the business or organization. Thus ultimately, the leader creates the business.

William Safire

Free enterprise is the practice of capitalism under representative government.[197] The concept and practice of free enterprise lies at the very heart of the "American Dream." The organization's leaders are the "agents" establishing the organizations "climate" and determining whether the climate promotes or inhibits ethics.[198] The organization's climate refers to "How we do things around here;" in other words, the ground rules which determine proper and improper conduct by the business or organization's employees. The organization's ethics, or lack of them, determines the organization's long-term success, and the success of the implementation of the ethics is directly related to the level of trust between and among the leader and employees.[199] The relationship between ethics and values are correlated. Rokeach's defines an organization's value system as: "an enduring belief of the organization concerning preferable modes of conduct or end-states of existence along a continuum of relative importance."[200] The important points of this definition are; first values are beliefs, not facts; and second values are enduring, not transient; and finally values provide guidance to our mode of conduct and our personal goals. Both effective leaders and healthy organizations have an awareness of their core values.[201] Hitt and Rosen with Berger (1991) concur that one sign of a healthy organizational culture is congruence between the organization's statement of values and the daily behavior of its employees. Following are five indicators of an organization's congruence:

1. Harmony in values which provide a sense of "common" directions, that when operationalized establishes behavioral standards.
2. Harmony in values will provide the social energy, the esprit de corps, and the community which value people as the center of the organization.
3. Harmony in values permits leaders and senior management to influence employee/follower behavior without being physically present.
4. Harmony in values provides the "gyroscope" for managerial decisions.
5. Harmony in values provides a sense of stability and continuity during rapid change or chaos.

Successful leaders harmonize their values with their visions. Harmonious visions are highly attractive, are exciting, and exhibit absolute personal confidence in the leader's abilities to make extraordinary things happen. These leaders are aware that the creation of their visions requires persistence and the involvement of others. The creation of form from voice is hard work: requiring relentless effort, steadfastness, competence, planning, attention to detail, and encouragement.[202] Awareness that leaders and followers mutually influence each other, and only if there is a connection,[203] is crucial because leader's significantly influence which alternatives to issues are seriously considered and how alternatives are evaluated.[204]

Values in American work ethics historically have influenced business practices and principles as shown in Table 6. The 1995 Washington State Leadership Voices™ study of state elected and appointed officials, business executive officers, and community sages' values, proactive management principles and

Table 6. Evolution of American Work Ethics

John Calvin (1509–1564)	Max Weber (1904–1968)	Everett Hagen (Circa 1962)	Robin Williams 1988	1995 Leadership Voices™ Survey[206]
• Bible is rule of faith. • No free will after Adam's fall. • Justification by faith alone. • Gratuitous predestination. • Improvement of society. • Utilitarianism • Private property fundamental to social order.	• Work as a "calling." • Success is a sign of grace. • Self—monitoring of grace.	• Introduction of innovative personality.	• Achievement and success. • Moral orientation. • Efficiency and practicality. • Process and progress. • Material comfort. • Equality. • Freedom. • External conformity. • Science and rationality. • Nationalism. • Democracy. • Individualism. • Racism and group superiority themes.	• Integrity—71% • Family[207]—41% • God—40% • Truth—29% • Justice—21% • Equality—17% • Love—14% • Authenticity—13% • Duty—11% • Happiness and Success—7% each • Honor and Peace—6% each. • Influence—4% • Virtue—1%

work consciousness—most frequently stated that their controlling core values were integrity, family, and God.[205] This study also conclusively showed that:

- A transformational leader's voice cannot be greater than the sum of each employee's voice; leadership is a fluid consciousness that mentors, motivates, and summons the work community to produce, with excellence.
- Transformational leaders' spiritual or religious affiliations underscore their visions and ethics of care; apprehending their personal and collective voices, congealing collaborative consciousness, and exciting through insight;
- Leadership Voices™ are the synchronized energetic vibrations of the work community, incorporating diverse personal core values orchestrated by proactive management principles;
- Proactive management goes beyond honesty and sincerity, requiring discipline, balance, dominion, and congruence between core values and actions;
- Transformational leaders must comprehend that they, and those, to whom they delegate administrative authority, create their core values in the work environment.

Simply put transformational leaders and proactive management tenets run parallel to traditional American work ethics but differs in one important aspect. Transformational leaders and proactive management tenets recognizes that individual's need internal balance because the inter-connective consequences of individual spirituality, core values and business profitability define the work environment. Bullies, determinedly difficult people, and predators can only thrive in work environments that condone thus reward their verbal abuse and bad behaviors.

NOTES

165. Hammond, Joshua and James Morrison, Stuff Americans Are Made Of: Seven Cultural Forces That Define Americans—A New Framework For Quality, Productivity And Profitability. (Simon and Schuster Macmillan Company: New York, 1996), ix.

166. Hammond, Stuff Americans, 3–6.

167. Irby, L. (2002) See Table 2: Summary of Literature Review's Terms and Phrases Connoting Transformational Leadership Values.

168. Ford, Leighton, Transforming Leadership: Jesus' Way of Creating Vision, Shaping Values and Empowering Change. (InterVarsity Press: Downers Grove, Ill., 1991), 405.

169. Peck, M. Scott, A World Waiting To Be Born: Civility Rediscovered. (Bantam Books: New York, 1993). Peck, M. Scott, The Different Drum: Community-Making

and Peace. (Simon and Schuster: New York, 1987). Ford, M. Scott, *A World Waiting To Be Born: Civility Rediscovered.* (Bantam Books: New York, 1993). Peck, M. Scott, *The Different Drum: Community-Making and Peace.* (Simon and Schuster: New York, 1987).1993 Parliament of Religions-Chicago. *Our Religions: The Seven World Religions Introduced By Preeminent Scholars from Each Tradition.* (Arvind Sharma (Ed.) Harper: San Francisco, 1993).

170. Ford, Leighton, Transforming Leadership: Jesus' Way of Creating Vision, Shaping Values and Empowering Change. (InterVarsity Press: Downers Grove, Ill., 1991).

171. Bouwsma, William J., *John Calvin: A Sixteenth Century Portrait.* (Oxford University Press: New York, 1988), 214.

172. Bouwsma, John Calvin, 197.

173. Weber, Max. (1995). *The Protestant Ethic and the Spirit of Capitalism.* Translated by T. Parsons. Introduction by A. Gibbens, Fellow of King's College, (Cambridge. Routledge: New York, 1995) xi.

174. Weber, The Protestant Ethic, xii.

175. Weber, The Protestant Ethic, 104.

176. Ford, A World Waiting, 74.

177. Ford, A World Waiting, 76.

178. Weber, The Protestant Ethic, 139.

179. Weber, The Protestant Ethic, 27.

180. Weber, The Protestant Ethic, xxi.

181. Weber, The Protestant Ethic, xxiii–xxvi.

182. Sztompka, Piotr, *The Sociology of Social Change.* (Blackwell, Oxford U.K. and Cambridge U.S.A., 1993), 237–240.

183. Sztompka, The Sociology of Social, 239.

184. Sztompka, The Sociology of Social, 240.

185. Sztompka, The Sociology of Social, 240.

186. Sztompka, The Sociology of Social, 241.

187. Sztompka, The Sociology of Social, 241–243.

188. Yankelovich, Daniel, New Rules: Searching for Self-Fulfillment in a World Turned Upside Down. (Random House: New York, 1981), 189.

189. Yankelovich, New Rules, 164–171.

190. Safire, William, Safari's New Political Dictionary: The Definitive Guide to the New Language of Politics. (Random House: New York, 1993), 451.

191. Walton, Clarence C., *The Moral Manager.* (Harper Business: New York, 1988), 57–58.

192. Walton, The Moral Manager, 1988.

193. Hess et al., 1988, pp. 175–176.

194. Adler & Towne, 1993; Hess et al., 1988.

195. Hess, Beth B., Elizeabeth W. Markson, and Peter J. Stein, *Sociology: Third Edition.* MacMillan (Publishing Company: New York, 1988).

196. Hess et al., Sociology, 70.

197. This term originally coined by President Roosevelt after the1936 Republican platform charged him with having displaced "free enterprise with regulated monop-

oly. The President's response to this allegation was: "Private enterprise, indeed became too private. It became privileged enterprise, not free enterprise," Not until 1944 did Roosevelt reaffirm his "faith" in the free enterprise system with his statement: "I believe in free enterprise—and always have. I believe in the profit system—and always have" (Safire, 1993).

198. Hitt, William D., *Ethics and Leadership: Putting Theory into Practice*. (Battelle Press: Columbus, Ohio, 1990), 2.

199. Hitt, Ethics and Leadership, 2.

200. Hitt, Ethics and Leadership, 7.

201. Kouzes, Kouzes, James. M. and Barry Z. Posner, *The Leadership Challenge: How To Get Extraordinary Things Done in Organizations*. (San Francisco: Jossey-Bass, 1987), 7.

202. Wheatley, Margaret. J. and Myron Kellner-Rogers, *A Simpler Way*. (Berrett-Koehler: San Francisco, 1996), 50.

203. Bennis, Warren G, *On Becoming A Leader*. (Addison-Wesley: Menlo Park, 1989), 104.

204. Irby, L. Irby Linda, Leadership Voices™ : Values, Proactive Management, and Consciousness. (UMI: 304 1369, 2002).

205. Leadership Voices™ survey respondent's values displayed in Table 3 are listed in order of frequency selected these totals will not add to 100%.

206. When the survey subgroups were analyzed separately: 1) Racial minorities responded that their three controlling core values were Family, Integrity, and Truth. 2) Women as a subgroup most frequently selected integrity, truth, and love as their three controlling core values. 3) The elected and appointed official's subgroup most frequently selected integrity, justice, and truth (Irby (2002), p. 184).

207. Mapes, *Quantum Leap*, 33–51.

Chapter Six

Leadership Operationalized

Our values are so much an intrinsic part of our lives and behavior that we are often unaware of them—or, at least, we are unable to think about them clearly and articulately. Yet our values, along with other factors, clearly determine our choices, as can be proved by presenting individuals with equally "reasonable" alternative possibilities and comparing the choices they make. Some will choose one course, others another and each will feel that his or her election is the rational one.

William Hitt

Leaders and managers need to understand political realities, organizational structures, symbols and culture. A healthy work environment has leaders and managers who are cognizant of the ever-increasing interdependence within our world's communities. A business' survival and success will only be achieved by the ability to abut diverse and seemingly incongruous core values within its work force when it's leaders:[208]

- Acknowledge their values (voice) create work standards, principles and the environment.
- Acknowledge their personal spiritual/religious affiliation.
- Acknowledge their personal values (voice) significantly influence their work ethics.
- Acknowledge their religious or spiritual values guide or support them in establishing and defining work policies and processes.
- Acknowledge their spiritual or sacred writings provide guidance when making management decisions.
- Acknowledge their religious or spiritual beliefs influenced their leadership or management style.

- Acknowledge their religious or spiritual belief influenced/defined their standard(s) for work productivity.
- Acknowledged their core belief(s) influenced their standards for productivity.
- Acknowledge that when they had control over budgets their basic philosophy was either "for the overall benefit of the business" or "bottom line" fiscal responsibility.
- Transformational leadership must be balanced with the practical experience that "situations" may require transactional management.
- Acknowledge they believe that "good" management principles are proactive to situations.
- Acknowledge that they "got what they asked for" so they strove to achieve balance between personal reflection and work outcome.

It must be remembered that everyone has at least one core value. Whether or not an individual's values have their basis in a religious or spiritual orientation of course will depend on the specific individual. However, research has shown that it is not coincidental that the preponderance of leaders who are Transformational Leaders acknowledged that their core values resonated from their religious and/or spiritual convictions. It is hypothesized that religious and/or spiritual convictions other than Christian are harmonious with Transformational Leadership. The focus on Christianity and proactive and transformational leadership is because the "the traditional American work ethic" is Christian.

PROACTIVE MANAGEMENT

An increasing number of scholars and business leaders concur that recent changes in the concept of business practices and organizational structures are paralleled by changes in the individual's philosophies.[209]

Early in the nineteenth century, the "self-made man" was revered because of his hard work, thrift, pluck, integrity, and perseverance. The self-made man believed he could do anything, and he had traditional values. After World War II, we saw the emergence of organizations and the "organizational man." He was motivated by achieving, or at least appearing to have, the correct "personality;" the correct social conformance, smile and effective small talk.

The baby-boom generation blazed the introspective review of traditional values and work ethic and "evolved" as the era of the "self:" a principle that asserted that reality is reflected in the help of "self." Thus we saw a shift from the self-made Man to the man-made self. Finally, contemporary individuals are being asked to make tremendous quantum leaps, in many cases, in their

personal concepts of "self," the kinds and nature of work, and their values that
determine their success. Individuals, who have been "established in the work
force," are being required to make what are often fundamental changes — very
rapidly. Generally speaking, individuals entering today's work force for the
first time are quickly acclimated, while "established workers" typically have
difficulty acclimating. The changing work environment is causing a clash between traditional work values and the contemporary work culture. Thus, Jo-
hensen and Swigart (1994) compare managers who use proactive management
principles to fisherman weaving and casting fishnets. In this metaphor, managers do have an effect, but they are pulling and rearranging fishnets through
their modeling, mentoring, and motivating their employees. The manager, in
the fishnet organization, may at one time be at the apex, at another in the middle. The inherent strength of the fishnet organization is its ability to rearrange
itself quickly while retaining its intrinsic stamina. The resulting tension and
conflict is often separate and in addition to the changes in technology. Many
observers of the changes occurring today in our workforce assert that some of
the fundamental cultural and work shifts occurring include:

1. Organizations are evolving from pyramid to fishnet[210] structures as hierarchy's collapse and broad, interwoven, flexible "fishnets" emerge.
2. Employees are increasingly self-reliant in providing health benefits, career
   planning and retirement benefits.
3. Businesses are increasingly becoming more focused on process than relationships. This intensified focus on process requires large investments of
   time and money being spent on adopting the basic principles of total quality management in order to better understand and improve their business
   processes.
4. Within organizations, individuals are more apt to participate in business
   teams and ad hoc alliances than large units or divisions.
5. Businesses (often both non-profit as well as for profit) are shifting their attention to customer service. Competitive analysis, still important, also
   identifies areas were cooperation is fiscally and resource prudent.
6. Electronic networks are replacing office buildings as the locus of business
   transactions. "Employees" are where their network is, so the nature of
   management supervision, facilities planning, and cost and supply and demand are drastically changing in all types of industries and provisions of
   service.
7. Diversity is a business reality in today's global market. The "traditional"
   us-versus-them mentality is yielding to the realization that the old majority is becoming a minority — and the employee or customer is often a
   member of the new majority.

8. Continuous learning rather than one-time training for "employees" is becoming the norm for competitive businesses and organizations. Today's efficient and productive work force must be flexible and capable of continually acquiring new skills. Learning must be life long and it is for everyone.
9. Simplistic notions of linear time (what have you done for me lately) are being replaced by complex concepts. These complex concepts acknowledge that management retains the right to control the nature, allocation and quality of work; but the terms of working conditions are often considered to be those of community. Often working conditions must be negotiated with labor organizations, employees, and team members.
10. There is a second half of adult life, age 50 and over. Individuals no longer "just retire," but move into an age of mastery with awareness and find their own voice. The impact of these voices, on communities as well as businesses, as employees/team members, stake holders, and customers is, and will continue to be significant in determining work values, ethics and productivity. These voices will also mentor others in determining their "core" values and measurements of personal success.

Proactive Management principles consist of the following elements:[211]

1. The ability to "be hungry" and embrace job insecurity. Leaders and managers, who succumb to the quest for job security, tend to escalate their paranoia. Increasingly, individuals who seek job security will find that there can never be "enough" job security.
2. The ability to address one's "power principle," remembering that the "point" of having power as a leader or manager is to seek the opportunity to be of service.
3. Demonstration of excellent collaboration skills between and among people and groups. The ability to bring others to consensus, however, must not be obscured by forfeiting principles, because the leader's or manager's opinion is in the (numerically) minority dissenting opinion.
4. Balancing "intellect" and "heart" in the decision-making processes, the conscious remembrance that at times, "all intellect will see is the double bind" in agonizing situations. Realizing that often it is the heart that will find the irrational consensus or solution to situations which otherwise seem intellectually obstructed.
5. Developing, maintaining and renewing trust, faith and self-assurance in one's leadership and management aptitude. Self-assurance diminishes the personal necessity, provoked by insecurity, to "prove" (to one's "self" or others) one's superiority or seek recognition.

6. Recognizing and comprehending that as leaders and mangers "you" determine the cultures of the organization. Your individual "voice" leads in the creation of the work environment by permeating your entire authorized span of "control."
7. Acknowledge that, as management, being isolated tempts poor choices or acts in judgment regarding confidants.
8. Appreciating that competence must be appropriate to the situation. Management competence should include several ways to access and use power, to include the following styles; authoritarian, consultative, participatory, and consensual.

Dealing with difficult people is an inherent part of being a supervisor, manager, and leader of people. How you, as a leader and manager deal with difficult people draws heavily on your competence and knowledge of an extensive range of skills and abilities acquired through academic study and experience. Continuous education and skills enhancement in the following areas, as displayed in the following Figure 6.1, establish the competencies necessary for effective leadership and management. Effectively balancing and integrating adult learning styles, anger management techniques, active listening and clear communication skills, and encouraging the heart and modeling the way takes patience, practice, and self-discipline. Dealing with difficult people over whom you have administrative authority typically is the nightmare of every supervisor, administrator, and executive officer. Where do you start, with those who immediately report to you and to whom you have delegated authority. There is a very good chance that most, if not all achievers whom have appointing and/or supervisory authority have the proverbial two faces. The thoughtful, "butter wouldn't melt in their mouth" mask that is shown to you and all "higher up's," and the megalomaniac face that everyone unfortunate enough to be enslaved by him cowers from. How will you know when you have this chameleon working for you? Pay attention: when you walk through the work area do you hear any laughter? If you stand still in the work area do you hear the sighs of despair? Have the number of suicide attempts, domestic violence incidences, work place violence, and frequency of unanticipated absences increased among your employees? Have the number of grievances, discrimination/harassment complaints, on the job injuries or continuous use of "leave without pay" plagued your workers? Have workers tried to arrange meetings with you to tell you about the verbal abuse, "secrete" defaming of character responses to job reference checks. If so then this supervisor or administrator is the tyrant and if you do not do anything your absence of action is equivalent to your approval and support of his actions. Paying attention to how you look, to your work force, through the eyes of your

Figure 6.1.   Essential Skills and Abilities for Leadership and Proactive Management.

Transformational Leadership, Proactive Management and Supervisory Skills	*Competencies*
Adult Learning Styles	• Basic understanding regarding diverse, interactive listening skills. • Basic understanding regarding diverse, interactive communication skills. • Basic understanding regarding need for affirming, clear communication. • Basic understanding in the diversity between genders in learning outcomes. • Use different communication methods and acknowledge special needs. • Basic understanding that staff will integrate their "learning" into more than one phase of their life. • Basic understanding that adults are performance outcome based in their learning and evaluations. • Basic understanding of adult motivation (related to learning).
Ancillary Services—Effective Use of	• Attorneys General • Auditor's • Division of Access and Equal Opportunity • Human Resource • Information System Services • Training
Anger Management—of "others"	• Recognize when they are threatened. • Recognize when they are weak. • Recognize when they are afraid. • Recognize when they are insubordinate. • Recognize when they are dangerous. • Recognize when performance is unacceptable.
Anger Management—Personal	• Recognize when you are dictatorial. • Recognize when you are repressive. • Recognize when you are strident. • Recognize when you are rigid. • Recognize when you are verbally abusive. • Recognize when you are fanatical.

Collective Bargaining	• Ability to clearly define process definition and guide lines regarding:
	  • Type of collective bargaining method
	  • Exchange of written initial bargaining contract.
	  • Etc.

(continued)

Figure 6.1.   *(continued)*

Transformational Leadership, Proactive Management and Supervisory Skills	*Competencies*
Communication 	• Ability to leverage past joint accomplishments to identify common ground in the current issue. • Ability to identify "real" issue. • Knowing that the first few moments set the climate for the "discussion". • Ability to identify the "nature" of the conversation—and any changes that may occur during the conversation. • Antagonistic • Dialogue • Informative • Motivational • Preservative • Something else??? • Ability to be clear about topic(s) of communication and desired outcome.
Compensation	• Ability to accurately classify job duties. • Ability to accurately identify distinguishing characteristics between various levels of jobs within same job classification. • Ability to prevent work "slippage" so that inadvertently employees do not perform work of a higher job classification. • Employees are compensated for their competence, skills, and abilities not favoritism.
Cost Benefit Analysis	• Ability to balance mandate for permanent performance excellence with dependable "average" performance. • Ability to balance loyalty to you and always being in agreement with loyalty to you and truthful expressions of dissent.
Counteracting Manipulative Behaviors	• Ability to recognize. • Ability to redirect. • Ability to address behaviors *not* infer intent.
Decision Making	• Ability to discern issue(s). • Ability to discern options. • Ability to discern desired outcome. • Ability to research necessary information for analysis and/ consideration. • Ability to multi-task. • Ability to synthesize analogous information.

Figure 6.1. *(continued)*

Transformational Leadership, Proactive Management and Supervisory Skills	Competencies
EEOC/AA Programs	• Know your personal biases and prejudices. • Know when to ask for help/advice. • Know when to "promise" confidentiality. • Know when to "keep your mouth shut". • Know who you can "share" confidences with. • Know what kinds of record keeping. • Know your "coping" skills strengths and weaknesses. • Know when to use informal, formal and progressive discipline.
Employee Recognition	• Ability to acknowledge individuals in the way they appreciate recognition. • Ability to coach corrective behavior and/or performance effectively. • Ability to know the names and at least one personal thing about them. • Ability to address "others" as individuals not as "staff" or "units".
Encourage the Heart and Modeling the Way 	• Ability to address team needs, jointly and as individual team members. • Ability to monitor and mentor relationship behaviors and productivity. • Ability to set and move boundaries, as appropriate. • Ability to facilitate coworker's flexible team responsibilities. • Ability to provide clear, consistent, achievable performance expectations.
Facilitating and Leading Organizational Change	• Facilitating minuscule work adjustments. • Facilitating flexible work teams. • Facilitating situational "leaders" among staff. • Facilitating broad organizational changes that may or may not directly affect you and your work unit.
Hiring Process	• Knowledge of diverse job announcement advertisement. • Knowledge of effective interviewing techniques. • Knowledge of appropriate background and other pre-employment investigations. • Knowledge of job classification being recruited.

(continued)

Figure 6.1.   *(continued)*

Transformational Leadership, Proactive Management and Supervisory Skills	Competencies
	• Knowledge of retention strategies and promotional abilities and opportunities.
Labor Relations	• Knowledge of contract law.
	• Knowledge of negotiation techniques.
	• Knowledge of clear writing techniques.
	• Knowledge of public speaking.
Leave	• Knowledge of the difference in rules between employees covered by a Collective Bargaining Agreement and those that are not.
	• Knowledge of the Family Medical Leave Act.
	• Knowledge of applicable Labor and Industries stipulations.
	• Knowledge of applicable use of leave as a reasonable accommodation.
Legal Issues	• Knowing your level of "fear" regarding legal entanglements.
	• Recognize a "suit" in the making.
	• Determine when are your employees operating "in the course of conducting business".
	• Knowing whom your legal support team is.
	• Ability to facilitate a common definition of trust within your work force.
Motivation	• Ability to develop and stimulate and sustain "trust".
	• Ability to capitalize on the momentum of high aspirations.
Negotiations in Everyday Situations	• Comprehend that typically a collaborative approach to creative problem solving works best.
	• Comprehend that "negotiation" *is* finding the middle ground.
	• Being aware that today's negotiation will affect the long-term relationship between parties—and among your team members.
	• Ability to identify all issues to be negotiated.
	• Ability to differentiate between negotiation content and negotiation process.

Figure 6.1. *(continued)*

Transformational Leadership, Proactive Management and Supervisory Skills	Competencies
	• Ability to identify all issues to be negotiated.
	• Ability to differentiate between negotiation content and negotiation process.
	• Comprehension that if either content or process are missing in the negotiation process, one of the parties *may feel emotionally cheated*.
Organizational Assessments	• Ability to continuously *change* organization *to maintain* stability.
Performance Counseling	• Ability to impartially evaluate employee performance against productivity standards.
	• Ability to clearly articulate, in advance, the distinguishing characteristics between exceptional, average, poor and unacceptable performance.
	• Recognize that if the employee does not feel good about their performance they will not feel committed to the job.
	• Appreciate that individuals know when you are lying about their performance—either over estimating or under-estimating.
Proactive Management Principles	• Know the difference between delegation and dictatorship.
	• Recognize and avoid "condemnation by too faint praise."
	• Perform strategic staff development—stop favoritism and ostracism.
Productivity, Excellence & Value Added	• Ability to actually hear staff's concerns.
	• Ability to communicate that you will or will not do something about staff's concerns.
	• Ability to discern when to let your employee "just be average' and quit trying to "motivate" them.
	• Ability to delegate.
Quality Control	• Recognize the connection between planning and achieving objectives.
	• Ability to blend diverse employee skills, learning styles and work processing.
	• Facilitate exploration of options.
	• Knowing the boundaries of each job classification?

(continued)

Figure 6.1.   *(continued)*

Transformational Leadership, Proactive Management and Supervisory Skills	Competencies
Rules, Regulations, Policies & Procedures	• Knowing the tasks necessary to accomplish the job, with value added. • Knowledge that strategic planning goes hand-in-hand with developing policies. • Knowledge that appropriate training and review of work related rules, regulations and policies is part of "forewarning" in "just cause" discipline. • Knowledge that verbal abuse (from you or from one of your employees) always violates some rule, regulation, policy or procedure. (Verbal abuse is always inclusive in harassment, discrimination, retaliation, stereotyping, and often a form of retaliation.

employees who "see you" in their supervisor and/or administrator can be a traumatic experience. The degree of your trauma is directly proportional to the "gap" that exists between how you "see" yourself, and how you are seen as presented through those to whom you have given administrative authority. Leaders not only have to personally "walk their talk" they have to ensure that those that follow "know the words" and "walk the talk."

Johansen and Swigart (1994), pertinently assess the impact that various technological levels of sophistication have on business and organizations. They point out that regardless of the level and degree of a business or organization's sophistication, globally they are increasing becoming economically interlinked and experiencing the compression of time and expanded expectations for quality. One response to the stress and competition induced by changes is the increasing assortment of quality improvement programs. The majorities of these programs are largely patterned after Edward Deming's (1986) model, and are rapidly becoming the primary "management theory" adopted by businesses and organizations. Edward Deming's premise for his continuous improvement through quality is succinctly stated in Neave's (1990) *The Deming Dimension*. Deming contends that quality and uniformity are foundations of commerce, prosperity and peace. Deming's philosophy of honoring the individual, while striving for uniformity and scientifically based improvement, is captured in his quality model's 14 Points, summarized as follows:

1. Constancy of purpose. Create constancy of purpose for continual improvement of products and service, allocating resources to provide for long-range needs rather than short-term profitability.
2. The new philosophy. We can no longer live with commonly accepted levels of delays, mistakes, defective materials, and defective workmanship.
3. Cease dependence on mass inspection. Eliminate the need for mass inspection as a way to achieve quality by building quality into the product in the first place, and by requiring statistical evidence of built-in quality in both manufacturing and purchasing functions.
4. End lowest-tender contracts. End the practice of awarding business only on the basis of price tag.
5. Improve every process. Constantly improve the system (the planning, production, and service), to improve every process, product or service quality, and productivity, thereby decreasing costs.
6. Institute training. Institute modern methods of training for everybody's job, including management, to make better use of every employee.
7. Institute leadership of people. Adopt and institute leadership aimed at helping people to do a better job.
8. Drive our fear. Encourage effective two-way communication and other means to drive out fear throughout the organization, so that everybody may work effectively and more productively for the company.
9. Break down barriers. People must work in teams to tackle problems encountered with products or service.
10. Eliminate exhortations. Eliminate the use of slogans, posters, and exhortations demanding Zero Defects and new levels of productivity without providing new or different process methods. The bulk of the causes of low quality and low productivity belongs to the system and, therefore, lie beyond the power of the workforce.
11. Eliminate arbitrary numerical targets. Eliminate work standards that prescribe quotas for the workforce and numerical goals for people in management by substituting aid and helpful leadership to achieve continual improvement of quality and productivity.
12. Permit pride of workmanship. Remove the barriers that rob hourly workers and people in management of their right to pride of workmanship.
13. Encourage education. Institute a vigorous program of education and encourage self-improvement for everyone.
14. Top management commitment and action. Clearly define top management's permanent commitment to ever improving quality and productivity and their obligation to implement all of these principles. It is not enough that top management commit themselves for life to quality and productivity, they must know what it is that they are committed to.

15. Deming's 14 points and other modified models of his quality programs attempt to continuously induce managers to engage in long range planning, reexamine basic assumptions about business programs, "scientifically" reassess production processes, and integrate formally separate components of business. However, a manager cannot lead:

    • without followers or employees,
    • despite situations or issues,
    • ignorant of multiple management styles,
    • contemptuous of diversity, or
    • void of core values.[212]

Regrettably, all too often the practical application of Deming's quality improvement model produces negative, unexpected or unintended results within the organization with morale, profits or productivity. This is especially true for those organizations that are not production oriented. Some of the probable causes of negative, often disasters results independently or jointly include:

1. The "quality" of the change agent introducing the program to the business or organization.
2. Inadequate modifications of Deming's model (initially developed for-profit production business) to non-profit service or government businesses or organizations.
3. One or more of Bolman and Deal's frames have been omitted or patronizingly attempted.

Bolman and Deal's (1991) *Reframing Organizations* emphasized that effective managers must balance the role of ethics and values, quality, commitment and creativity in today's competitive, contemporary organization. This balancing act is visually described as framing 4 core organizational elements:

1. The Structural Frame is bureaucratic or hierarchical in nature and emphasizes coordination and control to achieve effectiveness.
2. The Human Resource Frame has motivation and commitment as common process strands, which erupt the status quo in order to, integrate the individual and the organization.
3. The Symbolic Frame is most important in environments of ambiguity and uncertainty. Their primary purpose is to explain, and through rituals or slogans initiate individuals into the organization's culture or resolve confusion, increase predictability and direction. Here lies the business or organization's stories and myths that address morale, humor, play, metaphors, security, socialization, legitimacy, communication and community.

4. The Political Frame concentrates on manipulating the competition for power and the allocation of scarce resources. This frame is the conscious or repository of values and power.

MANAGEMENT CONSCIOUSNESS

Every day the number of leaders in various fields are voicing the same future occurrence the contemporary workforce is increasing more populated with employees that are most probably geographically dispersed and culturally diverse. A business or organization's team not only will have different professions, different values and different sets of skills; these teams most probably will be temporary in nature, lasting only the life of the project. This diversity of team locations and team member's interdisciplinary skills, cultural, ability and racial variance may create problems. The paradox, team heterogeneity is the critical element, which facilitates teams to respond to—and resolve problems in new, effective, productive, and balanced ways.[213] The contingency theory is a major sub-precept of systems theory. Systems theory begins by stating that every "thing" is a system of component parts. The nature of organizations is contingent on its function but depends on the nature of its parts.[214] Organizations will vary according to the nature of its component parts; if you change a part of the organization, the whole organization has to change. The whole organization has to change if only in relationship to the modified component.

With this enormous diffusion of power companies must quickly react to changes in the market place and shift accountability and authority into the hands of people who are closest to the products and the customers. That requires new business strategies and organizational structures. However, structures and strategies are not enough; this is where values come in. The more volatile and dynamic the business, the more the controls have to be conceptual, or it becomes the ideas of the business that control, not management. Values provide a common language for aligning a company's management and its people.[215] Today's culture means that organizations will change, whether they want to or not, to remain competitive. These changes are often chaotic to the individuals involved as well as the organization as a "system." The hierarchy, an element rapidly becoming obsolete, is flattening to webs of organizational ambiguity. Individual employees find they no longer have "career ladders:" instead they find planing their career is like crawling onto ropes, gasping for stability. The stability which employees so frantically attempt to grasp comes and goes quickly—if stability comes at all. There is no safety net.[216]

Chapter Six

Individuals now discover that "advancing in one's career" is a continuous process, not a move or decision. No longer can there be loyalty to a work unit, division, or an employer. The contemporary, competitive individual no longer thinks as an "employee" but as a "team player:" one who forms and reforms with other team-players, perhaps for a variety of organizations, committing to the task, not people.[217] This restructuring of the nature and kinds of "work" also means that the physical location of either the organization or the team members has less importance. "Virtual spaces" have significance and value because in hyperspace, greater and greater amounts of buying, selling and interpersonal exchanges are occurring.[218] Management's philosophy includes its values by how they prioritize their focus of attention, priorities, goals and policies of implementation.[219] Traditionally, management tends to fall into the following general classifications:

1. Attention is concentrated on financial or physical resources geared for long-range success.
2. Employees are viewed as opportunistic and self-interested, rather than trusting, while fiat or costly bargaining resolve conflicts.
3. Authoritarian (management) decision making occurs "top-down" (Theory X).
4. Decision-making occurs in a more participatory form from the "bottom-up" (Theory Y).
5. Management is more decentralized with flatter structures and fewer levels of management.
6. Employment is viewed as long-term, intensive socialization of employees with a clear statement of objective and values emphasizing cooperation and teamwork (Theory Z). The implication is the Theory Z form of management is a greater equalization of power and control from the "bottom-up." However, the equalization of power and control is not necessarily equivalent. Actually, Theory Z forms of management have mixed effects on senior management's power and control, but for the most part tends to increase their control. The decentralization and team decision making of Theory Z increase the equalization of power, but employee-organizational lifelong commitments may increase employee's tolerance for what ordinarily may be the subject of complaints. The emphasis on good human relations may reduce constructive confrontation; generalists career development may reduce the ability to move to another company; and the flatter Theory Z organizations eliminate middle managers who, in taller-structured bureaucracies, for example, filter and control what information gets to top management.[220]

An organization's community lives in the minds of its managers, employees, contractors, customers, and stakeholders, through shared assumptions, beliefs, customs and ideas. These shared values give meaning to ideas and motivation to community members. Among these shared ideas are the norms, that in a healthy and reasonably coherent community, people have derived by consensus.[221]

However, one of the observed shifts currently taking place are more and more managers are increasingly becoming conscious about their cause and affect on the organization. There tends to be three methods senior managers use to deal with this awareness:

1. Managers attempt to deny their "power or affect" on the organization by trying to hide the fact they have power and affect.
2. Managers attempt to become consciously charismatic, attempting to purposefully "seduce" or "manipulate" the organization at every possible opportunity.
3. Manager's recognition and alliance with tension.[222] (This is the only sustainable way this really works.) Only through the complex balancing act (mandated by organizational tension) will the managers be able to achieve their voice as servant leaders.

In addition to concerns that employees have abandoned traditional work ethics such as loyalty, there is an equally growing concern that some individuals lack organizational consciousness, indicated by their tendency to confuse businesses with families. An individual's inability to discern the difference between an organization and a "family" occurs when the following precepts of business are obscured:

1. Businesses hire and fire employees/members, families do not hire members.
2. Businesses do not have to hire an individual, there is no deserved employment, in families an individual does not have to demonstrate any level of competency to be or remain a member.
3. Businesses' primary "role" is to produce a marketable product, in families; the primary role is to "nurture" family members.[223]

PROACTIVE LEADERSHIP

Managers need a set of values to guide them in the selection of objectives. . .
Managers should make certain that the values guide the selection of objectives
and not allow the objectives to dictate the selection of values.

William Hitt

TRANSCENDENT PURPOSE

James MacGregor Burns in his 1978 work, *Leadership*, is the "father" of Transcendent Leadership, now commonly called Transformational Leadership. This newly coined leadership style elevated visionary leader's consciousness by power and effectiveness. Leaders induce followers to act for certain goals that represent the values and the motivations—the wants and needs, the aspirations and expectations—of both leaders and followers.[224] Power, a recognized and much discussed element of leadership, is essentially classified in the following terms:

1. Legitimate and expert power: closely linked to authority in organizations, occurs when accorded formal right to demand compliance from those who have the duty to obey. Usually there is also a psychological predisposition to "obey" rather than a conscious decision to defer to formal legitimacy.
2. Reward and punishment as power: generally speaking, the more senior the levels of leadership or management, the less effective are economic rewards and penalties. However, withholding respect, recognition, and affection from the leader appears to be most influential.
3. Referent power: is influence stemming from the leader's ability to influence esteem for or identification with, another person.

Burns' discussion of the various classifications of power is crucial because it leads to his defining two fundamentally different and distinctive leadership styles; value and use power. His groundbreaking distinctions between transactional and transformational leadership raised the personal awareness and social consciousness of leaders. Burns describes these two fundamentally different forms of leadership as:

Transactional leadership: occurs when there is a contractual exchange, a transaction, between individuals for something of value. Each party to the bargain is conscious of the power, resources, and attitudes of the other, recognizing each other as persons, with related purposes relative to the bargaining process. There is no relationship between the individuals beyond the bargaining process; there is no bid of leader or follower to a "higher" purpose.

Transformational leadership occurs: when individuals engage with each other so that both leader and follower raise one another to higher levels of motivation and morality. Follower's expectations are closely influenced by what leaders hold out as necessary, desirable, deserved, and possible.[225] Similarly, leaders link follower's individual power bases for mutual support and common purposes. "Transforming leaders ultimately becomes moral in that they raises the level of human conduct and ethical aspiration, of both leader and led, and thus there is a transforming effect on both."[226]

Leaders can help convert hopes and aspirations into sanctioned expectations. Expectations carry more psychological and political force than hopes and aspirations. They are more purposeful, focused, and affect-laden; the expectation is directed toward more specific and explicit goals, ones that are valued by the builder of expectations. As entitlements they carry a greater air of legitimacy; people expect what is rightfully theirs and are provoked or outraged when they do not receive it.

James Burnes

However, Transformational leadership is a double-edged sword; people can be transformed down, in destructive ways as well as up, lifting their level of achievement.[227] Ford finds the answers to two great ego problems of leadership are fear and the sense of inadequacy. Genuine leaders operate out of a sense of calling, not a sense of being driven. When there is a sense of identity, a security comes from knowing who one is. Leadership is not something one does but something one is. "Centered in any great leader's soul is a sense of transcendent purpose."[228]

The values and principles of transcendent leadership charge both leaders and their followers. The following Table 7 below compares and contrasts the proactive leadership principles of Burns (1978), Kouzes and Posner (1978), Bennis and Nanus (1985) and the Leadership Voices™ 1995 survey. It is significant to observe that all four proactive leadership principles emphasize that a leader's strategy stems from her mission and the transcendent purpose of her leadership is the best result for all individuals concerned. Another theme common to all four principles is the premise that the leader's conscious recognition of individuals (followers and those impacted by her leadership) and core values are fundamental to transforming and proactive leadership tenets.

SELF-AWARENESS
GENERATES and SUSTAINS:

- Authentic Voice

- Chaos Buffers

- Core Values

- Diverse Dialogue

- Detailed Visions

- Personal Visions

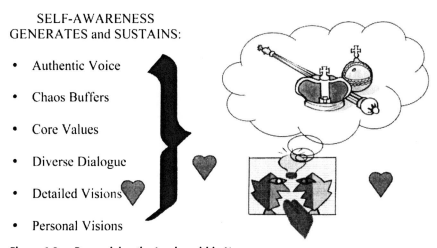

Figure 6.2.   Recognizing the Leader within You

Table 7.   Comparatives of Proactive Leadership Principles.

James M. Burns 1978	Kouzes and Posner 1978	Bennis and Nanus 1985	Leadership Voices™ 1995
• Conscious of interrelated means and ends. • Pursue expansive goals and long-range purposes. • Realize "cost" and "benefits" of action(s) must be clear. • Information, correct and clear, is invaluable. • Assess impact of policies. • Anticipate reactions from stakeholders. • Extend empathy. • Anticipate dissent. • Use conflict deliberately to maximize options. • Use conflict to maximize "constructive" dissonance. • Include diverse opinions in making decisions.	• Search for opportunities. • Experiment and take risks. • Envision the future. • Enlist others. • Foster collaboration. • Strengthen others. • Set the example. • Plan small wins. • Recognize individual contributions. • Celebrate accomplishments.	• Be self-aware. • Synthesized visions. • Credibility. • Commitment. • Empowerment. • Commitment to learning. • Flexibility, ability to shift paradigms. • Clear communication. • Be accountable, predictable, and reliable. • Positive attitude. • Accept people for who they are.	• Enterprising, changing and transforming. • Budget philosophy—"overall benefit." • "Good" Management principles are proactive to situations. • Business "success" to be measured by standards. • Education is worth allocating training funds to. • Greatest value is influencing outcomes. • Aware personal values significantly influence work ethics. • Spiritual writings guide decisions. • Spiritual values guide defining work policies. • Spiritual beliefs influence management style. • Spiritual beliefs do not inhibit ability to lead.

A leader's strategy stems from her mission and great leaders have a transcendent purpose. Ford agrees with Bellah[229] that if only two percent of any nation has a new vision of what they would like their society to be, they can change that society.

1. Leaders must be conscious of interrelated means and ends when they act. Leaders and policy makers must be aware of the wider political environment which may be intrusive, hostile, and intractable, at many different levels, at various times, through informal and formal goals and lines of accountability.
2. Leaders must maintain the highest degree of flexibility in their roles. Leaders must work to support values and purposes that enable them to embrace long-term goals. The avoidance of multifarious institutional demands must be avoided.
3. Leaders must realize the costs and actions of anticipated benefits over the long run are unpredictable. Resist concentrating simply on method, technique, and mechanisms of process instead of focusing on the broader ends of purpose, programs, goals, or vision. Too often leaders must act within values, goals, interest, and needs which have a hierarchy or "altered" goal or value that the leader may not recognize.
4. Leaders must rely on information that is both correct and clear. If leaders had more and better information then they could exert more influence, however, the cost of gaining extensive, correct information relative to the time and resources spent is high.
5. Leaders must assess the impact of policies. In satisfying existing and recognizable needs, policies may in fact alter or extinguish the motivations of other policies. One act or omission can not be made without disturbing the equilibrium of something else, or, creating new, additional or different "wants and demands" somewhere else.
6. Leaders must anticipate reactions from stakeholders. Both formal and informal reactions from legitimate and unofficial leaders need to be anticipated for their reactions may vary the circumstances, structure or outcome from the leader's original presumptions.
7. Leaders must extend empathy. Leaders need to be able to comprehend and respond to cognitive and emotional needs and values of "others."
8. Leaders must anticipate dissent. Leaders who make decisions in a vacuum or without considering the impact of dissenters are irrational and often increase tensions that could have been avoided or lessened.
9. Leaders must conflict deliberately to maximize options. Leaders should seize the opportunity to view conflict as a review of "old" ideas and concepts, and as possible indicators, that she should shift established paradigms.

10. Leaders must use conflict deliberately to maximize "constructive" dissonance. Conflict should be used to protect decision-making options and power, as well as structure the political environment, so that dissonance is seen in its most constructive light, for the most informed decision-making posture possible.
11. Leaders must maximize inclusion of diverse participants and ways to access systems. Systems should allow the access of multiple advocates, pluralistic problem solving, and thought processing into the decision making process. Pluralistic or multiple decision making processes allow the maximum range and variety of wants, needs, demands, values and purposes to be considered, yielding the best possible consideration of an issue.

Bass[230] states the difference between a transactional public leader and a transformational public leader is: one who "crystallizes" what the people desire, "illuminates" the rightness of the desire, and coordinates its achievement. However, such leadership can be transactional or transformational." There are almost as many different definitions of leadership as there are persons attempting to define the concept. However, he has been able to develop an approximate sense of classification for the concept of "leadership" as:

1. The focus of group processes.
2. A matter of personality.
3. A matter of inducing compliance.
4. The exercise of influence.
5. As particular behaviors.
6. A form of persuasion.
7. A power relationship.
8. An instrument to achieve goals.
9. An effect of interaction.
10. As a differentiated role.
11. The initiator of structure.
12. Any combination of the identified classifications.

Tension is created when an organization and its leader confront the awareness that the organization (and individuals comprising the organization) face reorganization or fundamental reshaping.[231] At this time the organization's leadership is the catalyst, the energy, the voice that initiates the change the keeps the organization:

1. Competitive[232]
2. Profitable[233]
3. Healthy[234]

Ford (1991) adds that a sense of timing is essential to leadership; a good leader is neither overly cautious nor impetuous. This sense of timing is best established by self-awareness. In addition to timing, the use of power requires both equilibrium and skill. Ford's previously discussed definition of power, as the ability to bring about through others the intended consequences. However, Ford equates more than one's position with power: he also includes information, knowledge, visibility, timing, trust, integrity, personal energy and self-confidence. To these attributes he adds showmanship, congeniality, access to the "inner circle," and the ability to obstruct or delay. Finally he concludes that winning is powerful and so is the ability to create the illusion of power. Of course power may be much more than just described, but whatever power is—power is not value-neutral. Power is value-driven.

The majority of people want leaders who are honest, competent, forward-looking, and inspiring: they want leaders who are credible and who have a clear sense of direction.[235] When successful leaders talked about their personal best achievements, they talk about searching for opportunities to innovate and change things. For these leaders, the real motivator is the challenge of the adventure, not the material rewards. These leaders have a sense of direction and a purpose beyond the moment; they are positive and expressive in their presentation of their personal agendas. Leaders foster collaboration and build effective teams, enabling others to be in control of their own lives. Successful leaders serve as models for what followers are expected to be and do. They build commitment through a process of incremental change and small wins, sustaining the commitment to achieve excellence by recognizing individuals and celebrating successes. When leaders are at their best they challenge, inspire, enable, model and encourage.[236]

Kouzes and Posner's research showed the five fundamental practices that effective leaders do to get extraordinary things accomplished as:

1. Challenge the process. Leaders are willing to step out into the unknown, take risks, innovate and experiment to find new and better ways of doing things. Leaders understand they may not necessarily be the individual who created or originated the new product or work process.
2. Inspire a vision. In many respects, leaders live their lives backwards, they see pictures in their mind's eye of what the results will look like before they start the project. Their clear image of the future pulls them forward, inspiring a shared vision with their followers.
3. Enable others to act. Leaders invoke others to act, they involve those who must live with the results and make it possible for good work to be done by encouraging collaboration and building teams. Teamwork goes far beyond the leader and his or her immediate subordinates. It includes peers, supervisors, customers, suppliers all those who must support the vision.

4. Model the way. Leaders must have detailed plans, performance measurements, funding, and the ability to take corrective action. Leaders also always
   keep in mind that their jobs give them authority, but their behavior earns
   them respect, earned through authenticity, and practicing what they preach.
5. Encourage the heart. Leaders must encourage the heart of their followers,
   because the creation of form from voice is hard work, and often time consuming.

Leadership is a transaction between leaders and followers because neither
can exist without the other.[237] However, they also consider self-regard as critical to effective leaders, for leaders see themselves as worthy, strong, nurturing, and disciplined. Leaders are discerning, enjoying their work, because it
satisfies their basic needs while reflecting their values. Additionally, this self-
awareness has the supplementary effect of creating a sense of confidence and
high expectations in others, akin to the Pygmalion effect.

Self-awareness resulting in positive self-regard develops emotional wisdom. The amount and degree of a leader's emotional wisdom is mirrored to
her by the way people relates to her. Bennis and Nanus found the five indicators of emotional wisdom include the following skills:[238]

1. The ability to accept peoples the way they are.
2. The capacity to approach relationships and problems in the present tense.
3. The ability to treat those close to you with the same amount of respect and
   courteous attention as strangers and casual acquaintances.
4. The ability to trust others, even when the risk appears great.
5. The ability to do without constant approval and recognition from others.

Ward (1965) conducted a large survey of CEOs in the United States, which
suggested that the religious affiliation of the top managers in a firm affected
the personnel policies promoted within the firm. His study indicated that personnel practices were more likely to be liberal when the top management was
not restricted to members of one religious group. When senior management
(CEOs) were exclusively Jewish, personnel policies tended to be liberal when
compared to exclusively Protestant senior management; the most conserva-
tive personnel policies being exhibited when senior management was exclusively Catholic. Bass (1990[239]) points out that once employed, each business
or organization's requirements determine the characteristics of members who
become and are accepted as leaders. The successful individual to emerge as a
leader, and to be evaluated as an effective leader, depends on the philosophy
of the organization. The effects of the organization's characteristics and philosophy also move successively down to the lower levels of management and

contribute to the constraints which are imposed, the structures that are created, the methods used to motive people, the resources allocated, and standards used for performance evaluations. All of these elements affect the leader-follower relationship in the organization.[240]

TRANSFORMATIONAL LEADERSHIP

People don't connect with other people to accomplish less. Behind all our organizing, is the desire to accomplish, to create something more. In this desire, we mimic the World. Life organizes to discover new varieties, different capacities. But in organizations, this organizing desire takes some strange forms. We want to generate more capacity but approach it through prescriptions and designs. We determine the levels of contribution we require and then design production roles. We try to engineer human contribution. We set clear expectations for performance. We then ask people to conform to our predictions about their contribution. We freeze them into their functions.

Margaret Wheatley and Myron Kellner-Rogers

Today's rapidly changing and uncertain conditions in values, technology and employment have made unprecedented demands on both business and our leaders. These unparalleled conditions are requiring a radical, sometimes fundamental rethinking by our leaders of their purpose, priorities and visions. Beckhard and Pritchard (1992[241]) identified the following 5 characteristics as the drivers of change, impacting both the organization and often the nature of work:

1. Change in the mission or "reason to be."
2. Change in the identity or outside image.
3. Change in the relationships to key stakeholders.
4. Change in the way of work.
5. Change in the culture.

To lead, one must separate old myths from current "standards," myths are the threads that link us to our past and shape our perception of the present and filter our "reality." Leaders who can not separate old myths from new realities, warns Jennifer James,[242] join exclusive clubs, withdraw from their communities and employees, easily justify wage disparities and remain unaware of the impact on production. Myths link us to our past and shape our perception of the present in the following ways:

1. Reinforce boundaries between individuals in a group—or separate one group from another.

2. Set schedules.
3. Provide models for productivity.
4. Are clues to the way a culture views or adapts beliefs to fit reality.
5. Attach themselves to all of life's crises.
6. Filter what is happening to us through our existing beliefs.

Peck (1993[243]) implores leaders or senior managers to recognize that personal isolation (at the top) tempts poor choices or acts in judgment regarding confidants. Poor judgment is more than "like selects like" or "birds of a feather flock together." Reflective confidant selection breeds either the best or the worst aspects of the leader's personality. This is particularly import to remember since the leader or senior manager determines the culture and sets the tone (usually unconsciously) for the entire organization.

James (1996) suggests, that future thinking leadership skills include: assessing individual and corporate interdependencies; self-reflection; appreciating, acknowledging and employing symbols and myths; and finally being sensitive to corporate culture.

Bennis (1989) likens defining leadership to defining "good" art, "It's hard to define, but you know it when you see it." Hershey and Blanchard (1977) contended that leadership is situational, a series of tasks, and that ideal leaders were both assertive and concerned about others. They were among the first respected researchers to contend that leaders deal with conflict by integrating conflicting ideas through collaborative problem solving. They pioneered the view that the best leaders are both highly concerned for production and highly concerned for people and can integrate the two.

Bass's (1990) discussion of Friedler's contingency theory of leadership stressed those leadership characteristics or traits most probably depended on situations. Friedler's theory differed from other "Great Man theories" in that he did not attempt to define leadership by characteristics, attributes, or the maturity level of the leader's followers. There is always implied action in leadership, even if the action is considered one of mentoring, coaching, or counseling. While Terry (1993) and Simons et al. (1993) stress that a leader must be authentic and regard diversity; courage, incorporating diversity, interdependence, interdisciplinary dependency and community are considered necessary for competent leadership.[244] As depicted in the following Table 8: Leadership Tendencies, the literature agrees the characteristics of Transformational Leaders are:

1. Able to avoid "taking sides" by offering new "possibilities" which are synthesized two or more contentions.[245]
2. Able to move beyond pointless conflicts and avoids one-sidedness.[246]

Table 8. Leadership Tendencies

Transactional Leadership Tendencies	Transformational Leadership Tendencies
Self-disguised.	Self-aware.
Create other's visions.	Visions create.
Do things "right."	Do the "right" things.
Communications veil.	Communications connect.
Trust is irregular.	Trust is habitual.
Incongruent voice.	Balanced voice.
Work within situations.	Change situations.
Accept what can be talked about.	Change what can be talked about.
Accept rules and values.	Change rules and values.
Talk about payoffs.	Talk about goals.
Bargain, "this for that."	Symbolize, what is mutually beneficial.
Motivates by enticements.	Motivates by raising awareness.

3. Able to bridge the "obvious" with integrated interests/consciousness and provide a perspective other than one, which is purely personal.[247]
4. Able to transcend one's personal psychological attitude, typically enabling objectivity and the routine negotiation of feasible solutions.[248]

The Transformational leader's enlightenment, ability and strength to balance the demands of work and personal life, fuse his awareness resulting from introspective comprehension and collaborative follower's voices. The Transformational leader's simultaneous awareness of his sacred values, proactive management principles and community consciousness is the energy that transmutes the leader's ability to have the perspective, which includes others.

The transformational leader's ability to be aware of "others" creates a new synthesis of work cultures, values, excellence, and productivity. Thus, when leaders know and appreciate that their voice is energy and energy creates form, then they will transcend their personal voice, knowing it can not be greater than the sum of their employee's individual voices. The collective voices, of both leader and followers, are the Leadership Voices™ which synthesize the organization's sacred values, proactive management principles and community consciousness.

CHANGE MODELS

Enlightened leadership can change cultures by changing the assumptions on which cultures are built. The leader who does this must have knowledge of the existing culture and be aware of the organization's key concerns. Leaders and managers need both the awareness and skill to determine what induces change and which of the many change models is appropriate for the change outcome desired. Some of the better known change models include but are not limited to the selected following examples:

1. Chaos Theory. Autry (1991) asserts that it is not the system that produces mistrust, it is the human interaction between management and employees that contributes to mistrust. Martin and Meyerson (1988) advocate a multi-paradigm viewpoint when assessing an organization from a cultural aspect. Morgan (1989) points out that every organization has its own story, and its stories indicate the organization's style, core values and daily routine. Senge (1990) endorses learning organizations that invite balance, induce community and assist those involved in the change to accept and appreciate the chaos of change. Wheatley (1992) offers the theory that disorder (chaos) can be a source of order and that growth is in imbalance, not balance. The unpredictability of the system is one of dynamic of connnectedness, so, given enough time, one can see the patterns. The key is to analyze how a workplace organizes its relationships not its tasks.

2. Building Trust and Communication. Bridges (1991) recommends that information be given to people clearly, concisely, and often. Hall and Thompson (1980) recognized that the ideal manager is a servant leader who empowers their staff to become team members and to maximize their strengths and individual contributions to achieve team goals. Ryan and Oestreich (1991) identify four areas that evoke fear in employees: abrasive and abusive conduct by managers, ambiguous behavior by managers, poorly managed personnel systems, and organizational cultures which place emphasis on performance and conduct of "top" managers.

3. Teamwork Models. Drucker (1988), views future organizations as being "information based" and organized into "task-focused" teams. Lawler et al. (1980), contend that the decision to use teams must recognize that teams are time consumptive. Therefore, when using teams it is important to put in sufficient time for (team) development, function, process and performance. Morgan (1989) supports internally directed, autonomous work groups, centered on multifunctional individuals and multidisciplined groups addressing issues in a holistic and integrated way. Sundstrom et al. (1990) developed four types of temporarily formed, interdependent work teams; advice, production, project and action: to be established contingent on need. Torres and Spiegel (1990) contend that self-directed teams were best when there is a commitment to improving the work process. Tuckman (1965) and later Petrock (1990) both analyzed team development and identified distinguishable and predictable stages in the development of teams. Both Tuckman and Petrock appear to agree on the following necessary states in the building of teams; forming, norming, storming, producing and ending.

NOTES

208. Irby, Linda, Leadership Voices™ : Values, Proactive Management, and Consciousness. (*UMI: 304 1369*, 2002), 182–186.

209. Doyle, William, and William Perkins, Smash the Pyramid: 100 Career Secrets From America's Fastest-Rising Executives. (Warner Books: New York, 1994). James, Jennifer, Thinking in the Future Tense: Leadership Skills for a New Age. (Simon and Schuster: New York, 1996). Jamieson, David, and Julie O'Mara, Managing Workforce 2000: Gaining the Diversity Advantage. Forward by Warren Bennis. (Jossey-Bass: San Francisco, 1991). Johnansen, Robert and Rob Swigart, *Upsizing the Individual In The Downsized Organization: Managing in The Wake Of Reengineering, Globalization, And Overwhelming Technological Change.* (Doddison-Wesley Publishing: New York, 1994). Mapes, James. J., *Quantum Leap Thinking: An Owner's Guide to the Mind.* Dove Books: Beverly Hills, 1996). Naisbitt, John. And Patricia Aburdene, *Megatrends 2000: Ten New Directions for the 1990's.* (William Morrow And Co., Inc.: New York, 1990). Popcorn, Faith, *The Popcorn Report: Faith Popcorn on the Future of Your Company, Your World, Your Life.* Doubleday Currency: New York, 1991). Sheehy, Gail, *New Passages: Mapping Your Life Across Time.* (Random House, Inc.: New York, 1995).

210. The fishnet is a metaphor Johansen and Swigart (1994) chose to express the form contemporary, competitive organizations are materializing. In this metaphor, managers do have an effect, but they are pulling and rearranging fishnets. The manager, in the fishnet organization, may at one time be at the apex, at another in the middle. The inherent strength of the fishnet organization is its ability to rearrange itself quickly while retaining its intrinsic stamina.

211. Covey Steven R., Principled Centered Leadership: Give A Man A Fish and You Feed Him For A Day; Teach Him How To Fish And You Feed Him For A Lifetime. (Simon and Schuster: New York, 1992). Greenleaf, Robert. K., Servant Leadership: A Journey into the Nature of Legitimate Power and Greatness. (Paulist Press: New York, 1982). Peck, M. Scott, A World Waiting To Be Born: Civility Rediscovered. (Bantam Books: New York, 1993), 250–268.

212. Aziz, Robert, C.G. Jung's Psychology of Religion and Synchronicity. (State University of New York Press, 1990). Bass, Bernard M., Bass and Stogdill's Handbook of Leadership: Theory, Research and Managerial Applications. (The Free Press: New York, 1990). Bolman Lee G. and Terrence E. Deal, *Reframing Organizations: Artistry, Choice, and Leadership.* (Jossey-Bass: San Francisco, 1991). Forbes, Beverly A. (1991). *Profile Of The Leader Of The Future: Origin, Premises, Values And Characteristics Of The Theory F Transformational Leadership Model.* Unpublished manuscript. Seattle, Wash., October 1993. Ford, Leighton, *Transforming Leadership: Jesus' Way of Creating Vision, Shaping Values and Empowering Change.* (InterVarsity Press: Downers Grove, Ill., 1991). Gardiner John. J. and Beverly A. Forbes. *Preparing Effective Leaders For An Interdependent World: Seattle University's Multidisciplinary Doctoral Cohorts.* Paper presented to the National Leadership Group of the American Council on Education, Washington, D.C. December 3, 1993. Hall Brian P. and Helen Thompson, *Leadership Through Values,* (Paulist Press: New York, 1980). Walton, Clarence C., *The Moral Manager.* (Harper Business: New York, 1988).

213. Bennis, Warren G, *On Becoming A Leader*. (Addison-Wesley: Menlo Park, 1989). Cox, Warren G, *On Becoming A Leader*. (Addison-Wesley: Menlo Park, 1989). Eisler, Riane., *The Chalice and The Blade: Our History, Our Future*. (Harper: San Francisco, 1987). Farson, Richard, *Management of the Absurd: Paradoxes in Leadership*. (Simon and Schuster: New York, 1996). Forbes, Beverly A. (1991). *Profile Of The Leader Of The Future: Origin, Premises, Values And Characteristics Of The Theory F Transformational Leadership Model*. Unpublished manuscript. Seattle, Wash., October 1993. Gardiner John. J. and Beverly A. Forbes. *Preparing Effective Leaders For An Interdependent World: Seattle University's Multidisciplinary Doctoral Cohorts*. Paper presented to the National Leadership Group of the American Council on Education, Washington, D.C. December 3, 1993.Gilligan, Carol, *In A Different Voice: Psychological Theory and Women's Development*. (Harvard University Press: Cambridge, 1993). Gleick, James, *Chaos: Making A New Science*. (Penguin Books: New York, 1987). Greenleaf, Robert. K., *Servant Leadership: A Journey into the Nature of Legitimate Power and Greatness*. (Paulist Press: New York, 1982).Gretz Karl. F. and Steven R. Drozdeck, *Empowering Innovative People*. (Prous Publishing Company: Chicago, 1992). Hall Brian P. and Helen Thompson, *Leadership Through Values*, (Paulist Press: New York, 1980). Hitt, William D., *Ethics and Leadership: Putting Theory into Practice*. (Battelle Press: Columbus, Ohio, 1990). James, Jennifer, *Thinking in the Future Tense: Leadership Skills for a New Age*. (Simon and Schuster: New York, 1996). Johansen Robert and Rob Swigart, *Upsizing the Individual In The Downsized Organization: Managing in The Wake Of Reengineering, Globalization, And Overwhelming Technological Change*. (Doddison-Wesley Publishing: New York, 1994). Kiersey David and Marilyn Bates, *Please Understand Me: Character and Temperament Types*. (Prometheus Nemesis: Del Mar, Cal., 1984). Kouzes James. M. and Barry Z. Posner, *Credibility: How Leaders Gain And Lose It, Why People Demand It*. (Jossey-Bass: San Francisco, 1993). Mapes, James. J., *Quantum Leap Thinking: An Owner's Guide to the Mind*. Dove Books: Beverly Hills, 1996). Naisbitt John. And Patricia Aburdene, *Megatrends 2000: Ten New Directions for the 1990's*. (William Morrow And Co., Inc.: New York, 1990). Peck, M. Scott, *The Different Drum: Community-Making and Peace*. (Simon and Schuster: New York, 1987). Peters, Tom, *Thriving On Chaos: Handbook For A Management Revolution*. (Alfred A. Knopf: New York, 1988). Peters, Tom, *The Pursuit Of Wow: Every Person's Guide to Topsy-Turvy Times*. (Random House, Inc.: New York, 1994). Popcorn, Faith, The Popcorn Report: Faith Popcorn on the Future of Your Company, Your World, Your Life. (Doubleday Currency: New York, 1991). Sheehy, Gail, *New Passages: Mapping Your Life Across Time*. (Random House, Inc.: New York, 1995). Terkel, Studs, Coming of Age: The Story of Our Century By Those Who've Lived It. (The New Press: New York, 1995). Terkel, Studs, Coming of Age: The Story of Our Century By Those Who've Lived It. (The New Press: New York, 1995). Terry, Robert. W., *Authentic Leadership: Courage in Action*. (Jossey-Bass: San Francisco,1993). West, Cornel, *Race Matters*. (Beacon Press: Boston, 1991). Wheatley, Margaret J, *Leadership and The New Science: Learning About Organization from an Orderly Universe*. (Berrett-Koehler: San Francisco, 1992). Wheatley, Margaret. J. and Myron Kellner-Rogers, *A Simpler Way*. (Berrett-Koehler: San Francisco, 1996). Wiley, Ralph., *Why Black Peo-*

ple Tend to Shout: Cold Facts and Wry Views From a Black Man's World. (Penguin Books: New York, 1991).

214. Peck, A World Waiting, 35.

215. Compilation (Harvard Business Review, 1992), 35.

216. Johansen, Ralph., Why Black People Tend to Shout: Cold Facts and Wry Views From a Black Man's World. (Penguin Books: New York, 1991), x.

217. Johansen, Why Black People, x.

218. Johansen, Why Black People, x.

219. Bass, Bernard M., Bass and Stogdill's Handbook of Leadership: Theory, Research and Managerial Applications. (The Free Press: New York, 1990), 571–572.

220. Bass, Bass and Stogdill's, 572.

221. Bolman, Lee. G. et. al., *Leading With Soul: An Uncommon Journey Of Spirit.* (Jossey-Bass: San Francisco, 1995).

222. Greenleaf, Robert. K., Servant Leadership: A Journey into the Nature of Legitimate Power and Greatness. (Paulist Press: New York, 1982). Peck, , M. Scott, A World Waiting To Be Born: Civility Rediscovered. (Bantam Books: New York, 1993). 1993; Senge, 1990.

223. Peck, M. Scott, *A World Waiting To Be Born: Civility Rediscovered.* (Bantam Books: New York, 1993), 196–197.

224. Burns, James M, *Leadership.* (Harper and Row: New York, 1978), 19.

225. Burns, Leadership, 118.

226. Burns, Leadership, 20.

227. Ford, Leighton, Transforming Leadership: Jesus' Way of Creating Vision, Shaping Values and Empowering Change. (InterVarsity Press: Downers Grove, Ill., 1991), 31–33.

228. Ford, Transforming Leadership, 52.

229. Bellah, Robert N. et al, Habits of the Heart: Individualism and Commitment in American Life. (Harper and Row: New York, 1985). Ford, Leighton, Transforming Leadership: Jesus' Way of Creating Vision, Shaping Values and Empowering Change. (InterVarsity Press: Downers Grove, Ill., 1991).

230. Ford, Transforming Leadership, 23.

231. Senge, Peter, *The Fifth Discipline.* (Doubleday: New York, 1990). Beckhard Richard, and Wendy Pritchard, *Changing the Essence: The Art Of Creating and Leading Fundamental Changes in Organizations.* (Jossey-Bass Publishers: San Francisco, 1992).

232. Compilation (Harvard Business Review), 1992; Hitt, William D., *Ethics and Leadership: Putting Theory into Practice.* (Battelle Press: Columbus, Ohio, 1990). James, Jennifer, *Thinking in the Future Tense: Leadership Skills for a New Age.* (Simon and Schuster: New York, 1996). Johansen Robert and Rob Swigart, *Upsizing the Individual In The Downsized Organization: Managing in The Wake Of Reengineering, Globalization, And Overwhelming Technological Change.* (Doddison-Wesley Publishing: New York, 1994). Peters, Tom, *The Pursuit Of Wow: Every Person's Guide to Topsy-Turvy Times.* (Random House, Inc.: New York, 1994). Schmidt, Schmidt, John E, Transformational Leadership: The Relationship Between Consciousness, Values and Skills (Leadership). (*DIA, 54(11A), 4057,* 1993). Simons et al., Simons, George F., et al. (1993). *Transcultural Leadership: Empowering the Diverse Workforce.* Gulf Publishing

Company: Houston. Terry, Robert. W., *Authentic Leadership: Courage in Action*. (Jossey-Bass: San Francisco,1993). Yankelovich, Robert. W., *Authentic Leadership: Courage in Action*. (Jossey-Bass: San Francisco,1993).

233. Bennis, Robert. W., *Authentic Leadership: Courage in Action*. (Jossey-Bass: San Francisco,1993). Burns, James M, *Leadership*. (Harper and Row: New York, 1978). Gardner, John W, *On Leadership*. (The Free Press: New York, 1990). Header, John, *The Tao of Leadership: Leadership Strategies for A New Age*. (Bantam Books: New York, 1985). Kouzes James. M. and Barry Z. Posner, *Credibility: How Leaders Gain And Lose It, Why People Demand It*. (Jossey-Bass: San Francisco, 1993). Weisbord, Marvin R., *Productive Workplaces: Organizing and Managing for Dignity, Meaning, and Community*. (Jossey-Bass: San Francisco, 1987).

234. Ford, Leighton, Transforming Leadership: Jesus' Way of Creating Vision, Shaping Values and Empowering Change. (InterVarsity Press: Downers Grove, Ill., 1991). Greenleaf, Robert. K., Servant Leadership: A Journey into the Nature of Legitimate Power and Greatness. (Paulist Press: New York, 1982). Hall Brian P. and Helen Thompson, Leadership Through Values, (Paulist Press: New York, 1980). Oakley Ed and Doug Krug, Enlightened Leadership: Getting to the Heart Of Change. Fireside: New York, 1991). Rosen, Robert with Lisa Berger, The Healthy Company: Eight Strategies to Develop People, Productivity and Profits. (Jeremy P. Tarcher/Perigree: New York, 1991).

235. Kouzes, Credibility, How, 1.

236. Kouzes, Credibility, How, xix.

237. Bennis, On Becoming, 32.

238. Bennis, On Becoming, 55–69.

239. Bennis, On Becoming, 571.

240. Bass, Bass and Stogdill's, 571.

241. Bass, Bass and Stogdill's, 37.

242. Beckhard, Richard, and Wendy Pritchard, *Changing the Essence: The Art Of Creating and Leading Fundamental Changes in Organizations*. (Jossey-Bass Publishers: San Francisco, 1992), 76.

243. Jennifer, Thinking in the Future Tense: Leadership Skills for a New Age. (Simon and Schuster: New York, 1996), 258–260.

244. Peck, M. Scott, *The Different Drum: Community-Making and Peace*. (Simon and Schuster: New York, 1987). Terry, Robert. W., *Authentic Leadership: Courage in Action*. (Jossey-Bass: San Francisco,1993). West, Cornel, *Race Matters*. (Beacon Press: Boston, 1991). Wheatley, Margaret J, *Leadership and The New Science: Learning About Organization from an Orderly Universe*. (Berrett-Koehler: San Francisco, 1992).

245. DePree, 1989, 1992, Forbes, 1991; Gardiner & Forbes, 1993; Greenleaf, 1982; Johansen, Robert and Rob Swigart, Upsizing the Individual In The Downsized Organization: Managing in The Wake Of Reengineering, Globalization, And Overwhelming Technological Change. (Doddison-Wesley Publishing: New York, 1994). Locke, Ewin A., et al., The Essence of Leadership: The Four Keys to Leading Successfully. (Lexington Books: New York, 1991). Peters, Tom, The Pursuit Of Wow: Every Person's Guide to Topsy-Turvy Times. (Random House, Inc.: New York,

1994). Simons, George F., et al., *Transcultural Leadership: Empowering the Diverse Workforce*. Gulf Publishing Company: Houston, 1993).

246. Edelman & Crain, 1993, Fisher & Ury, 1981; Ford, 1991; Heider, 1985; Hollander, 1978; Oakley & Krug, 1991; Terry, Robert. W., *Authentic Leadership: Courage in Action*. (Jossey-Bass: San Francisco,1993). Roberts, Wess, *Leadership Secrets of Attila the Hun*. (Warner Books. New York, 1990). Wheatley Margaret J, *Leadership and The New Science: Learning About Organization from an Orderly Universe*. (Berrett-Koehler: San Francisco, 1992).

247. Bennis, Warren G, *On Becoming A Leader*. (Addison-Wesley: Menlo Park, 1989). Cox, Warren G, *On Becoming A Leader*. (Addison-Wesley: Menlo Park, 1989). Kouzes, James. M. and Barry Z. Posner, *The Leadership Challenge: How To Get Extraordinary Things Done in Organizations*. (San Francisco: Jossey-Bass, 1987). Mapes, James. J., *Quantum Leap Thinking: An Owner's Guide to the Mind*. Dove Books: Beverly Hills, 1996). Samuels et al., Aandrew, et al., *A Critical Dictionary of Jungian Analysis*. (Routledge and Kegan Paul LTD: New York, 1993).

248. Burns, James M, *Leadership*. (Harper and Row: New York, 1978). Cohen, Herb, *New Perspectives On Negotiating*. (Harper Collins Publisher, Inc.: New York, 1993). Dilenschneider, Robert. L., *Power and Influence: Mastering the Art of Persuasion*. (Prentice Hall Press: New York, 1990). Goleman, Daniel. (1995). *Emotional Intelligence: Why It Can Matter More Than IQ*. Bantam Books: New York. Gretz Karl. F. and Steven R. Drozdeck, *Empowering Innovative People*. (Prous Publishing Company: Chicago, 1992). Jaworski, Joseph. (1996). *Synchronicity : The Inner Path Of Leadership*. Berrett-Koehler Inc.: San Francisco. James. M. and Barry Z. Posner, *Credibility: How Leaders Gain And Lose It, Why People Demand It*. (Jossey-Bass: San Francisco, 1993). Rusk, Tom. (1993). *The Power of Ethical Persuasion: From Conflict to Partnership at Work and In Private Life*. Penguin Books: New York. Ury, William, *Getting Past No: Negotiating With Difficult People*. (Bantam Doubleday Dell: New York, 1991).

Chapter Seven

The Synthesis of Values, Proactive Management and Community Consciousness

Our society has tried to establish a floor below which no one will be allowed to fall, but we have not thought effectively about how to include the deprived more actively in occupational and civic life. Nor have we thought whether it is healthy for our society to give inordinate rewards to relatively few. We need to reach common understandings about distributive justice — an appropriate sharing of economic resources — which must in turn be based on conceptions of a substantively just society. Unfortunately, our available moral traditions do not give us nearly as many resources for thinking about distributive justice as about procedural justice, and even fewer for thinking about substantive justice.

Robert Bellah

The synthesis of one's values, proactive management principles, and consciousness is the touchstone for change, building a healthy work environment and thus neutralizing bullies, determinedly difficult people and predators at work. When respect for others includes using a variety of clear communication styles, all individuals are then encouraged to authentically participate in the work community. Inclusive, authentic communication stimulates the creating and sustaining a work community that, through collaboration, has established common work values, visions, and performance excellence standards. This work community evolves into a team that comprehends and values each member's role as informal leader when needed.

Since each individual's voice is energy and energy creates form, there is power in communication. This communication, one's voice, when internally consistent with one's intent always manifests form. The key elements here are of course:

1. one's intent,
2. one's active clarity in receiving communication from others,
3. one's ability to clearly articulate to others, and finally
4. one's ability to transcend self-centered, survival excessiveness and consider shared gratification.

The power of communication, the ability to elicit collaboration, absorb and transmit motivational energy, and achieve desired outcomes is exhilarating. When you have fully heard and comprehended what is said to you, made an appropriate response that is thoughtful and authentic you then align your energy to fully encompass all desired, coincidental, and serendipitous occurrences. Practice increases your perceptions, your insight, your intolerance of verbally abusive and corrosive exchanges. Effective communication also means that you never verbally abuse another individual, particularly by assuming that you know what someone thinks or wants. Since your voice is energy, and energy creates form—and form (matter) can not be destroyed—remember what you say will always "be out there." So, when talking to yourself or others, your "voice" should be:

• Direct.
• Immediate.
• Clear
• Supportive
• Nonjudgmental
• Non-threatening.

One of the "creations" manifested by your words is your image of self and your perception others. Our self-concept over time matches the way we believe others see us thus the "self-fulfilling" prophecy of other's intentions and words toward us. Each of us tend to accept impressions that reinforce or basic identity and resist those that do not: unless there is a significant emotional event that alters basic self-concepts. So, your intent toward yourself and toward others daily manifests your attitude, motivates your behavior; and manipulates your wishes, hopes and desires.

VALUES CONSTRUCT VOICE, VOICE CREATES FORM

An increasingly expanding segment of dissertation research considers the interdependency between voice, values, transformational leadership, and proactive management. A review of pertinent contemporary research follows.

First, John Edwin Schmidt's (1993) dissertation, *Transformational Leader-ship: the Relationship between Consciousness, Values and Skills Leadership* examined leaders who appeal to "higher" values. Leaders who challenge in-dividuals, organizations and societies to make principled decisions that raise consciousness, transcend opposing perspectives, or serve the common good. This research investigated the nature of transformational leadership to learn what drives, motivates, and concerns leaders who facilitate transformation. This study showed that transformational leaders reflected a different "world view" or consciousness which was accompanied by a different set of values and skills (from Transactional leaders). Schmidt's study showed that trans-formational leaders reflected higher levels of consciousness, pursued differ-ent values, depended less on instrumental and interpersonal skills and used more imaging and systems skills Hall and Thompson's (1980) than did the comparison leaders who were

TRANSACTIONAL

Second, Kenneth Ruch's (1993) research, *Factors Influencing Performance in Manufacturing Work Systems: An Examination of Causal Relationships of Organizational Structure and Situational Workplace Variables on Proactive Management Behavior*, examined factors that influenced proactive work be-haviors of managers in manufacturing work systems. This work is ground breaking as it investigated the relationship between organizational structures and situational workplace factors and proactive/reactive work behaviors. The study's results showed a low but statistically significant relationship between organizational workplace factors and proactive work behavior. A manager's work behaviors can be correctly classified as either reactive or proactive based on organizational and situational factors, with situational activities pro-viding the strongest relationship to proactive work behavior.

Third, Stephen E. Jacobeans (1994) project, *Spirituality and Transforma-tional Leadership in Secular Settings: A Delphi Study*, considered how trans-formational leaders perceived the role of spirituality in their personal and pro-fessional life. Spirituality was defined as "a form of consciousness and activity in which the person is aware that they exist in a profound state of in-terconnectedness with all life and seek to live in a manner which nourishes and honors the relationship at all levels of activity." The study method was the creation of an international panel of nine experts, each of whom were asked to identify three to five leaders in secular organizations who embodied transformational traits. Twenty-two individuals participated in the study of the 43 that were nominated. The outcome of the study was that participants acknowledged that they understood their spirituality played a vital role in their personal and professional activities. When asked if they favored integrating their spirituality into secular organizational life, the responses of the participants varied. The majority of the participants were in favor of integration of spiritual propensities in their organizational life, but were cautious about what this would mean, particularly in terms of diversity.

Jacobean's study did indicate that there was a consensus in the sense that the term "spirituality" included issues of values, transcendence and subjectivity. Some of the participants assumed that the qualities of spirituality were essential to the creation and maintenance of an organizational atmosphere that was conducive to creativity, ethical behavior and "meaning-making." At the time of his study, there had been no major empirical studies that explored the question of the connection, if any, between a leader's ability to have a "transformational" effect on the organization and the leader's disposition toward spirituality. Interestingly, Jacobean's study emphasizes the element of love as an essential quality of transformational leaders. And, until 1995, only one other research project[249] explored the connection between transformational leaders and the role of spirituality or faith in the individual's life experience.

Diana Walling's (1994) research in *Spirituality and Leadership* was published the same year as Jacobensen's. Her research consisted of the researcher's personal, qualitative interviews with ten people that had leadership experiences. The study participants, five men and five women, were interviewed with regard to what, if any, relationship existed between their leadership and their spirituality. The study indicated there is a significant relationship between a person's spiritual journey and their leadership experiences, sometimes the relationship is intentional and other times it is part of the individual's core values. This research showed that an individual's spirituality (defined as the process of moving away from an egocentric existence to one that appreciates and values a reality greater than what is purely human) does not guarantee a more effective leadership. Jacobensen (1994) found there is a mutually enhancing relationship between an individual's spiritual journey and his leadership moments. The research's outcome is that the leader's awareness of his spirituality enhances his leadership in decision making, vision formation, attitude toward others, personal reflections, and commitment to an identified cause.

Walling's (1994) study asserts that spirituality influences the vision formation that is necessary to leadership. It also affects the attitudes that leaders take toward others in the leadership process. Moments of decision making, especially in times of crisis, often finds the leader seeking aid through whatever spiritual disciplines she follows. The reflection that is involved in leadership is shaped by her spirituality, if any. The ability to get outside one's own perspective is also enhanced by spirituality, helping a leader to stay committed to the cause. Finally, the relationship between leaders and followers cannot be fully explained without a spiritual dimension. The dynamic that makes leadership happen is influenced, not only by the spirituality of the individuals, but also by the relationship taking on its own spirituality, which can and does influence the process.

Fifth and finally William Effler's (1994) *Leadership by God's Design: Spirituality for Leadership's Personal and Corporate Growth* dissertation concluded that, "Any leader who practices "leadership by God's Design" would make better decisions, increase the effectiveness of their followers and enjoy a deeper personal spirituality. The supposition supported by this work is that God's Design consists of the leader following the "modeling" of God, does not "lord over" others.

Successful companies may have very different values and the values of one successful company, if capriciously assumed by another company, may in fact hurt another company. However, Kouzes and Posner,[250] point out that the most effective companies have three qualities in common:

1. Clarity. People know what their company stands for. While clarity is important, if there is no consensus about the values then operationally the organization has no authenticity; in other words it is perceived as not truthful, it does not "walk its talk."
2. Consensus. People understand the values and share in agreement with them. There is a high degree of commitment to what the leader and the organization stand for. Every organization has a set of values and principles by which it does business.
3. Intensity. Both the leader and followers feel solidly about the worthiness of their values so that there is: (a) A substantial degree of congruence between values and actions; and (b) An almost moral dimension to the necessity of "keeping the faith." In companies where there is a high level of shared values, the values are frequently major topics of conversation and there is some sort of monitoring system to ensure values and actions are congruent.[251]

Simply put, traditional American business practices are founded on Christian values. However, Christian values among and between Christian denominations vary (much less between those who's core values are based on something other than Christianity), thus the wide variation in business practices, management styles, and product/service delivery. Regardless of your personal religious/spiritual affiliation (or lack of one), if you were raised in America, you have had continuous and repetitive exposure to "traditional" work values, expectations, and productivity norms and mores. Thus, conflicting values—especially if the value is a "core value" to one or both parties—may be "the" origin triggering and sustaining the antagonism between you and your nemesis. The more closely your differences result from core values the more intense the "hostilities" between you and your nemesis.

Margaret Wheatley's (1992) *Leadership and the New Science* addressed the "springing forth of parallel concepts," that often seem to "spontaneously" appear in widely separated locations or from several disciplines at once.[252] She further states that the movement towards participative management is perhaps subconsciously rooted in changing perceptions of the organizing principles of the universe.[253] The Washington State 1995 Leadership Voices™ study's findings coincide with previous studies.[254] The majority of the *1995 LEADERSHIP VOICES*™ survey indicated that survey participants did have spiritual or religious propensities, and they did consciously attempt to balance their core values in both their personal and business lives. Survey individuals saw their roles as leaders as being participative, interconnected, and transforming.

INTERDEPENDENCY BETWEEN VALUES AND TRANSFORMATIONAL LEADERSHIP

Some critics have seen the "work ethic" in decline in the United States and a "narcissistic" concern with the self-emerging in its place. In our conversations, we have found that an emphasis on hard work and self-support can go hand in hand with an isolating preoccupation with the self, as Tocueville feared would be the case. Indeed, work continues to be critically important in the self-identity of Americans, closely linked to the demand for self-reliance. The problem is not so much the presence or absence of a "work ethic" as the meaning of work and the ways it links, or fails to link, individuals to one another.

Robert Bellah

Transformational leadership ultimately becomes moral in that leadership typically raises the level of human conduct and ethical aspiration of both the leader and the followers, and thus it has a transforming effect on both. The most admired leaders speak unhesitatingly and proudly of "our" mutual ethical aspirations. They know that "we" want to live up to the highest moral standards. So the first requirement of enlisting others is that leaders find and focus on the very best that the culture shares in common; on what the culture-group, organization, or nation means to its members. This communication of purpose, this commemoration of our dreams, helps to bind us together; it reminds us of what it means to be a part of this collective effort. It joins us together in the human family.[255]

For this reason, among others, leaders are obligated to make sure that followers know what they stand for and what the organization stands for. Followers who know and comprehend the leader's values and are able to align their personal values with the leader and are more likely to work hard to achieve the goals. Values are comprised of the things most important to us, the deep-seated, pervasive standards that influence almost every aspect of our lives, moral judgments, responses to others and commitments to personal and organizational goals. "However silently, values give direction to the hundreds of decisions made at all levels of the organization every day with values constituting our personal "bottom line.""[256]

Because values are intangible and "deep-seated" we never actually "see" values. What we "see" are the indicators of an individual's values manifested in their; opinions, attitudes, preferences, desires, fears, actions, strategies and so forth. It must be emphasized that leaders, like most people, are multidimensional, and so are their values.[257] The leader's values extend to many areas which include; prioritization of activities; personal needs for achievement and affiliation; locus of control; preference for risk taking; cooperativeness—competitiveness; trust and general well being. Additionally, the balance of assailant values tends to be similar in profit and non-profit businesses.

However, as one rises administratively, values tend to shift; and this shift in values generally can not be attributed to age, education or seniority.[258] Status differences and commitment to the organization tends to increase with one's administrative authority. First level supervisors, who tended to emphasize the importance of consideration and fairness, were less critical of subordinates and identified more with their work groups/subordinates than more senior management.

CHRISTIAN TENETS AND TRANSFORMATIONAL LEADERSHIP

The juxtaposition of the Christian's "call" to leadership is important in our tradition as it relates to "work," comes from the Old Testament (Deut. 7:7–8a).[259] The "call" is a covenant relationship: a "commission" to be a blessing to others. The "transforming" style of leadership has significant precedence in the church, for both the Old Testament prophets and Jesus were often in that role. The prophets called for repentance and new life, appealing to their congregation's identity as people of God, who were called to be a blessing to the nations of the world.

The concept of being called to leadership, from today's church viewpoint, is a call to a position, a relationship and action.[260] Christian leadership is often considered to be a ministry when it works in the service of others because it renews and brings about new life. The six essential functions of a Christian leader to are:

- clarification and maintenance of the vision:[261]
- "Where there is no vision, the people perish" (Proverbs 29:18, KJV),
- affirming the values of the organization,
- symbolizing the standards and expectations of the organization, a personification of the organization's vision and commitments,
- seeing that the organization is provided for, maintained,
- serving the organization, helping it to be an organization that serves, and
- working toward renewal, ensuring the organizations existence through change and responsiveness.

Leighton Ford (1991) notes that, as we become increasing aware of the world's changes, a major shift in leadership is crucial. Our postmodern world is exponentially experiencing enormous accelerations in changes. Ford contends a "transforming" leader is able to divest himself of power and invest himself in his followers.

INTERCONNECTED: TRANSFORMATIONAL LEADERSHIP AND PROACTIVE MANAGEMENT

The more present and aware we are as individuals and as organizations, the more choices we create. As awareness increases, we can engage with more possibilities. We are no longer held prisoner by habits, unexamined thoughts, or information we refuse to look at.

Margaret Wheatley

Hall and Thompson (1980) did considerable research into the parallel phases of consciousness and the stages of value development of leaders. Their work determined that a leader's consciousness becomes actualized through new values and the development of skill, of which there are four types; imaginal, instrumental, interpersonal and systems: each tend to develop at specific phases of consciousness. Therefore, the seven leadership styles identified by his study can be described in terms of the skills associated with the values and consciousness of the persons in the leader role. However, of even greater significance than the leadership styles is understanding that the consciousness-value-skill development process enables one to create conditions to develop new leadership styles. These new leadership styles most closely approximate the prophetic vision, voiced in level seven of their eight stages of consciousness. Thus in Figure 7.1, we see the "transformation" of the individual in her leadership stewardship, her management competencies, her social consciousness, and her spiritual awareness.

Hall and Thompson's leadership consciousness levels 1, 2 and 3: all of these leaders (Alienated Man, Preservation Man and Organizational Man) tend to be autocratic in leadership style. At the first level the individual "adapts" to his or her environment, by the third level the individual assumes internal authority and exercises critical choice, although awkwardly. Here, simply put, the leader is alienated, a tyrant who dictates to his or her followers. What distinguishes the leader from the domineering person at this first level is the domineering person's preoccupation with "power over" others and his or her preoccupation with achieving his or her goals by means of positional or personal power. This element of "power over" is one of the primary contributors of verbal abuse.

At Level 2 (Preservation Man), the leader-follower relationship resembles that of parent to child. Leaders tend to listen only if they feel others will incorporate their suggestions in the decision; only if, he or she feels his or her ideals will prevail as the final decision. Followers are expected to be blindly obedient. When a follower breaks his or her relationship with the leader, the action is seen as "personal treachery."

Finally, at Level 3 (Organization Man), the leader is the "benevolent paternalist" demanding loyalty to the organization. This leader is goal conscious, concerned with efficiency but usually kind. The instrumental skills associated with leadership at this stage are highly developed proficiency in

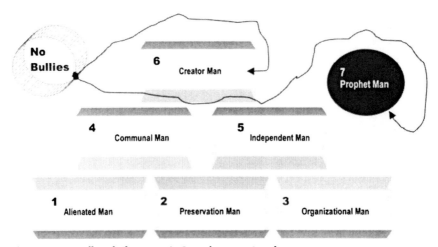

Figure 7.1.   Hall and Thompson's Consciousness Levels

technical skills such as; communications, data processing, bookkeeping, and marketing. There are the learned interpersonal skills of coping with conflict, remaining calm in high-stress situations, the identification of one's own feelings, and the ability to share emotion quickly and to handle anger objectively.

Level 4: Level 4, Communal Man, is a pivotal level. The leader has grown dissatisfied with his role as an organizational person. This leader is caught between loyalty to the institution and independence. It is in the transition from Level 3 to Level 4 that the Laissez-fare leadership style is adopted by individuals whose vision has begun to include the values of Level 3 (administration membership, accountability, competence and so forth), but they have yet to actualize the skills. It is at this level that the leader often confuses "belonging" and "being me," thus confusing relationships between work associates and the need to share intimately with friends. It is also at this level that the concept of "peer" emerges. It is at this level that the leader is most prone to clarify and support but never confront or make a decision. The leader may entertain new ideas but the leader will never initiate new projects. What is important to understand, is that the leader who has had bad experiences or harsh interactions with business or institutional leadership tends to remain at this level. However, a good experience at this level provides the leader with two visions about future organizational leadership; the first, institutions can be both efficient and caring; and second, leadership at its highest level is always plural. At this pivotal level, if and when this leader regresses he or she tends to regress to Level 1 or 2. On the other hand, it is at this level that the leader can make a conscious choice to grow and move to Level 5. Movement to Level 5 requires the authority be earned in light of each new experience, whereas previously it was given to the individual by virtue of position.

Levels 5 and 6: This is the third of Hall and Thompson's four phases of consciousness (Level 5, Independent Man and Level 6, Creator Man) and represents the independent person with a newly acquired sense of personal authority. This leader is self-directed and considers the world a place of invention and projects that must be creatively embraced. The internalized values exhibited at this level include self-assertion, independence, empathy, generosity and service. Here too, the leader begins to actualize the skills of innovation, construction, accountability, mutual responsibility and accomplishment of missions and goals.

It is at Level 5 that the leader is met with the necessity to have a "leap of consciousness" (or quantum leap) to achieve a systems awareness. The "leap" occurs when the leader becomes aware that Level 5 is possible and then learns the system skills to realize it.

Level 6 is very different from the previous levels because here the leader recognizes that leadership must be plural. It is at this level that "interdependence and harmony are the two values inherently necessary for collegial authority."

Here the leader is a facilitator of interdependent peer resources. The values of accountability, mutual responsibility, supportive community and construction have been internalized and the leader has the skills to handle aggression in a caring way. It is at this level that the servant leader emerges because concurrent proficiency and integration of the leader's instrumental, imaginal, interpersonal, and system's skills are equally developed.

Interesting enough, Hall and Thompson's research has shown that it is at this level of increasing professional competence, that the individual becomes aware they must be more in touch with their bodies. Thus dieting, physical exercise, fasting and relaxation are now essential to the leader's development. Here it is essential to realize that when the body is in tune, self-aware and there is balance and integration of family and professional life, then the quantum leap to Level 7 is possible.

Level 7: At this level, the fourth and final phase of consciousness (Profit Man), the leader has transcended to become a servant leader, the leader who has equal ease experiencing personal authority as unique and the development of new imaginal skills. Here the leader's cognitive skills are commensurate with the complexity of the position's responsibility. The leader at Level 7 is "the creator man" or—the individual who creates his (or her) vision's form from his (or her) voice.

It is important to note that while Hall and Thompson's work discussed the experience of leadership as developmental, what was meant is that the levels were sequential, and most probably reversible. In other words, their research showed that an individual's good experiences of leadership, even if experienced as a follower, provided the best basis for successfully developing to a higher consciousness level. However, bad experiences of leadership thwarted, perhaps even perverted development. While an individual's development is sequential there is nothing to show that environmental circumstances will not force a leader to regress to an earlier consciousness level.[262]

INTERCONNECTED: TRANSFORMATIONAL LEADERSHIP AND CONSCIOUSNESS

We will need to stop describing tasks and instead facilitate process. We will need to become savvy about how to build relationships, how to nurture growing, evolving things. All of us will need better skills in listening, communicating, and facilitating groups, because these are the talents that build strong relationships. It is well known that the era of the rugged individual has been replaced by the era of the team player. But this is only the beginning. The quantum world has demolished the concept of the unconnected individual. More and more relationships are in store for us, out there in the vast web of universal connections.

Margaret J. Wheatley

The American economy is demanding from the American worker a more stringent approach to life. At the same time, Americans are leaving behind the excess of the "me" decade, new rules of living are supporting self-fulfillment through deeper personal relationships, more enduring commitments to the world of work.[263]

Today most jobs are still constructed to reflect the traditional work picture; full-time, five-days-a-week, regular-hour jobs, with pay and fringe benefits based on the assumption that the jobholder is the sole earner in the family. However, this traditional work picture is rapidly changing as more part time, contract and self-employed individuals work with no benefits or limited basic benefits. We can expect vast changes in the future in how paid work and childcare are organized.[264]

In order for today's leaders to lead today's workers, the leader must transcend their own personal voice, knowing that it can not be greater than the sum of her employees/followers individual voices. In this way the collective voices of both the leader and followers are the leadership voices which synthesize the organization's sacred values, proactive management principles and community consciousness.

The attainment of consciousness through self-awareness requires the acknowledgment and comprehension of "others" being interconnected. Achieving and sustaining one's self–awareness requires balancing all aspects of one's life with communal consciousness. Community consciousness is achieved through one's religious or spiritual propensities, personal reflection and discipline. For a significant number of Americans, their acknowledged "faith" is Christianity.

Christian tenets have been shown to regard one's vocation, one's life work as the individual's "calling." Whether or not Christians who are in the workforce are indeed active in their calling is the topic of other research. What is pertinent in this discussion is the use of the secular word "vocation." Typically, Americans use this word to describe employment. The word "vocation," derived from the Latin verb "vocair," literally means "calling" and implies a relationship.[265] The secular definition of vocation usually implies only income-producing activity[266] while the religious meaning of the word encompasses an individual's fulfillment of "doing" (often very specific activities) by answering the "call" of God.[267] There tends to be the implied expectation that those who "answer" God's call invariably succeed, but not necessarily in stereotypical measurements of success if the "call" relates to employment.[268] If the "call" is resisted then the individual tends to experience various intensities of "dis-ease" which may prolong the individual's personal or career renewal, revitalization or transformation.[269]

Power, the capacity to influence others, is the most potent factor in organizational behavior. The misuse of power, incivility, most often occurs in management. The focus on managers occurs because this group of employees typically possesses the bulk of political power within an organization/business. Peck's (1993) *A World Waiting To Be Born,* contends that the spiritually incompetent manager will, inevitably, abuse power; consequently, the civil use of power in business should be the subject for management's consideration.[270]

> Briggs & Stratton Corporation have filed a $30 million libel and invasion-of-privacy lawsuit against the National Catholic Reporter. The reason, the National Catholic Reporter's commentary asserted, that Briggs "decision makers" (among whom are "Catholics educated in Catholic institutions) have breached moral conduct when they decided to layoff workers.[271]

This article indicated that the National Catholic Reporter's Mr. Fox hoped his commentary would spark a dialogue on whether executives should consider their religious principles when deciding tough corporate issues (such as layoffs).[272] The challenge to today's leaders and managers in organizations is to identify the following questions within their organizations and derive effective, productive, healthy methods for resolutions:

1. How do leaders and managers excite through insight with authenticity yet strategically wield power?
2. How do leaders and managers know when the system under their administrative control is stable and predictable?
3. How do leaders and managers attain simplicity and awareness amidst organizational changes and flexibility?
4. How do leaders and managers "follow" in "fishnet" organizations and still transcend their voice to synthesize the organization's sacred values, proactive management principles and community consciousness?
5. How do leaders and managers apprehend personal and collective voices yet remain serendipitous to synchronous occurrences creating their intent?

Yet, even when the leader has both a clear vision of the future and practical methods to resolve issues, she must be ever mindful that her vision can not be established by edict, exercise of power or coercion.

> Installing a vision is more an act of persuasion, of creating an enthusiastic and dedicated commitment to a vision because it is right for the times, right for the organization, and right for the people who are working in it.[273]

Visions most often are best communicated by metaphor, modes or "stories." So, the leader must consistently act on his vision, personalize it and repeat it time and again. The vision must be incorporated in the organization's culture and reinforced through the strategy and decision making process, constantly being evaluated for modifications resulting from new data or circumstances.

But, most importantly, for a vision to become form, the vision must grow out of the needs of the entire organization.

The entire discussion of a leader's voice/vision, the organization's goals, and the systemic productivity "rewards" are intrinsically interwoven with the leader's sacred values. Moreover, if the leader's values happen to be Christian based (as is the traditional American Business Ethic), then Leighton Ford's (1991) thoughts regarding vision are appropriate. Ford explains that in the Scripture the word vision is commonly used to describe how saintly people, with an awareness of God, received His word through an ecstatic experience. Vision is the stuff of leadership, it is the ability to see in a way that compels others to pay attention. Visions elicit something, from us, a response that "calls" us. In other words, vision is the seeing power of faith.

Faith enables us to see with our mind and imagination what we do not yet see with our eyes and experience. Vision is at the heart of one's great conviction. A leader's vision should be unconstrained, in other words, looking for the best in human potential. Visions can, and must be both unconstrained and realistic in order to transcend to the enormous possibility of human change by God's power. Ford described visionaries as individuals, who have a way of seeing and perceiving reality which may either be the seeing of extraordinary things or "simply" bring a new perspective to commonplace things which have been taken for granted.

VALUES, VISION, VOICE: ALL IS ONE

This is the reality we live: aspiring to be at our best, longing for and sometimes finding meaning and connection within ourselves and with that which is larger than ourselves, . . . Because beneath the small daily trials are harder paradoxes, things the mind cannot reconcile but the heart must hold if we are to live fully: profound tiredness and radical hope; shattered beliefs and relentless faith; the seemingly contradictory longings for personal freedom and a deep commitment to others, for solitude and intimacy, for the ability to simply be with the world and the need to change what we know is not right about how we are living.

Oriah Mountain Dreamer

Covey counseled, "Begin with the end in mind," so this discussion ends with the roots of transformational leadership in mind. Calvin's social thought highlighted his concern for community. For Calvin, wealth was given by God to meet the needs of community, notably those of its neediest members. Calvin was concerned with work and the use of both wealth and time, chiefly because he saw them as scarce resources for meeting community needs.

God has joined and united us together so that we might have a community, for men should not be separate. It is true that our Lord has ordained that each man may have his household, his family, his wife, and his children. So that each man will have his station, but no one may be exempted from the community so that he can say, I will live for myself alone. That would be to live worse than a beast. What then? We should know that God has obligated us to one another to help each other; and at least, when we see anyone in need, although we cannot do him the good we would like, that we treat him humanly. It is too great a cruelty on our part if we see a poor and afflicted man and do not try to help him, but rather turn away from him.[274]

The synthesis of sacred values, proactive management principles, and community consciousness form both the individual and collective elements of Leadership Voices™, we have stepped back to the future. Wheatley and Keller-Roger's thoughts on interconnectedness encapsulate our collective, increasing awareness regarding our interdependence.

The simpler way summons forth what is best about us. It asks us to understand human nature differently, not optimistically. It defines us as creative. It acknowledges that we seek after meaning. It asks us to be less serious, yet more purposeful, about our work and our lives. It does not separate play from the nature of being.[275]

Perhaps bullies, determinedly difficult people, and predators are as "natural" to human interactions as the vision of harmonious co-existence is to futurist. Humans have achieved both their best characteristics and their worse in the course of building and sustaining communities. So, as each of us becomes aware that our voice creates form, civility towards each other becomes ingrained as the minimal acceptable work interactive behavior. Our human collective consciousness has not shifted, our attentiveness and appreciation of consciousness is exponentially awakening, one individual at a time. Voice is energy, energy creates form.

NOTES

249. Marinoble, R. M., *Faith and Leadership: The Spiritual Journeys of Transformational Leaders*. Doctoral Dissertation, (The University of San Diego, 1990).

250. Kouzes, James. M. and Barry Z. Posner, *Credibility: How Leaders Gain And Lose It, Why People Demand It*. (Jossey-Bass: San Francisco, 1993), 195.

251. Kouzes, Credibility, How Leaders, 195.

252. Kouzes, Credibility, How Leaders, 139.

253. Wheatley, Margaret J, Leadership and The New Science: Learning About Organization from an Orderly Universe. (Berrett-Koehler: San Francisco, 1992), 143.

254. Schmidt, John E, Transformational Leadership: The Relationship Between Consciousness, Values and Skills (Leadership). (*DIA, 54(11A), 4057,* 1993). Schmidt, John E, Transformational Leadership: The Relationship Between Consciousness, Values and Skills (Leadership). (*DIA, 54(11A), 4057,* 1993). Jacobean, Stephen E., *Spirituality and Leadership in Secular Settings: A Delhi Study.* (Seattle University, 1994). Walling, Dana M. (1994). Spirituality and Leadership. *DIA, 55* (7A), 1783 . Effler, William B. (1994). *Leadership By God's Design: Spirituality For Leadership's Personal And Corporate Growth.* DIA, 55(6A) 1600.

255. Kouzes James. M. and Barry Z. Posner, *The Leadership Challenge: How To Get Extraordinary Things Done in Organizations.* (San Francisco: Jossey-Bass, 1987), 118.

256. Kouzes, The Leadership, 191.

257. Bass, Bernard M., Bass and Stogdill's Handbook of Leadership: Theory, Research and Managerial Applications. (The Free Press: New York, 1990), 140.

258. Bass, Bass and Stogdill's, 161.

259. Harris, W. Lee, *Effective Church Leadership: A Practical Sourcebook.* (Augsburg Fortress: Minn., 1990), 22–23.

260. Harris, Effective Church, 1990.

261. Harris, Effective Church, 1990.

262. Hall & Thompson, 1980, p. 64.

263. Yankelovich, Daniel, New Rules: Searching for Self-Fulfillment in a World Turned Upside Down. (Random House: New York, 1981).

264. Yankelovich, New Rules, xv.

265. Peck, M. Scott, *A World Waiting To Be Born: Civility Rediscovered.* (Bantam Books: New York, 1993), 61.

266. Peck, A World Waiting, 66.

267. Peck, A World Waiting, 61

268. Peck, A World Waiting, 67.

269. Peck, A World Waiting, 71.

270. Peck, A World Waiting, 245.

271. "The Wall Street Journal," Volume 23, Thursday, August 1, 1996, column 4, "Are Layoffs Moral?"

272. "The Wall Street Journal," Volume 23, Thursday, August 1, 1996, column 4, "Are Layoffs Moral?"

273. Bennis, Warren and Burt Nanus, *Leaders: The Strategies for Taking Charge.* (Harper and Row: New York, 1985), 107.

274. Bouwsma, William J., *John Calvin: A Sixteenth Century Portrait.* (Oxford University Press: New York, 1988), 201.

275. Wheatley, Margaret. J. and Myron Kellner-Rogers, *A Simpler Way.* (Berrett-Koehler: San Francisco, 1996), 5.

Chapter Eight

Transformational Leadership and Proactive Management

String theory is the unified theory of everything. From one principle—that everything at its most microscopic level consists of combinations of vibrating strands—string theory provides a single explanatory framework capable of encompassing all forces and all matter. We will see that force particles are also associated with particular patterns of string vibration and hence everything, all matter and all forces, is unified under the same rubric of microscopic string oscillations.

Brian Greene

AFFIRMATIVE DEFENSES TO BULLIES, DIFFICULT PEOPLE, AND PREDATORS

Perhaps you have wondered why your nemesis just does not mind her "own business" and leave you alone? What is in it for her to meddle with you? Possibly, you think that if you could just understand the motivation behind harassing you, you could get your nemesis to stop harassing you. The reality is, your nemesis wants to keep you believing that she is rational and that at some point an understanding can be reached. Why? So you will keep attempting to rationalize with your nemesis and she will thus keep having power over you. Your nemesis' verbal responses and/or behaviors will never correlate with reality. In fact, being unpredictable is one of her abusive behaviors that keeps you off balance. So appealing to her to be compassionate, your attempting to be submissive or accommodating in some way, and your attempts to reason with her will all be unsuccessful. What will work?

Tell your nemesis to stop, or tell someone in your chain of command that you want your nemesis to stop.

- Tell your immediate supervisor, your human resource manager, your civil rights manager, your labor representative about your situation.
- Keep a journal about behaviors, statements, any documents relating to your mistreatment.
- Do not engage in conversations or discussions with your nemesis about how they abuse you.
- Meet your needs as best you can. Do not rely on co-workers for your support.
- Become financially independent as soon as possible. This may mean that your need to reevaluate you're your needs and your wants. Do you have to sell everything, move, get a second job?
- Protect your time at work, only communicate about work related issues. Emphasize your excellence, productivity, and customer service.
- Protect your personal space. Specify when you want to be alone. Be firm and clear when saying "no" when you have authorization to do so. You can still be "nice" and firm about protecting your space.

Remember that it is human nature to resist change, particularly since what you may be asking your nemisis to do is make some basic changes to his sustained habits and/or value system. Primarily each of us develops part of our ego by reflected appraisal (the expectations of others), and more likely than not each of us prefer to choose what we're going to do; not have a particular action or course mandated to us. Do you have administrative authority over this difficult employee? If so, the inherent power of your position means you have the tools to consider these elements and establish a behavior modification and/or corrective action plan:

- Limit the number of options available to this employee to no more than 3, and of the 3, make sure that one of them is undesirable to the employee.
- Set specific, quantifiable, clear deadline(s) for action.
- Do not negotiate non-negotiable work completion, standards, and behaviors.
- Capitalize on the individual's "natural" inertial. People in motion tend to keep in motion.
- Remember, people tend to accept impressions that reinforce a basic identity and to resist those that do not. So, the law of expectations states that we need to speak and act directly.
- Show the employee that the task is "simple," achievable, and easy. After all, if the employee was not qualified for the job he would not have been hired.
- When appropriate use your progressive action program.

AFFIRMATIVE DEFENSES TO BULLIES, DIFFICULT PEOPLE, AND PREDATORS WHO ARE SUBORDINATES

Supervisors, according to Skinner (1965) have at least two dynamics occurring in their work areas behavioral and verbal, both of which can occur in social (group) dynamics and personal behavioral dynamics. While some social behavior may involve reinforcement, verbal behavior always involves social reinforcement.[276] Social stimuli are important to those that value social interaction, acceptance, and solidify their self-esteem.[277] Skinner discusses two types of "social episodes" that are relevant to our task of neutralizing work nemesis:

> Consider, for example, the interaction between predator and prey called "stalking." We my limit ourselves to that behavior of the predator which reduces the distance between itself and its prey and that behavior of the prey which increases the distance. A reduction in the distance is positively reinforcing to the predator and negatively reinforcing to the prey; an increase is negatively reinforcing to the predator and positively reinforcing to the prey. . . . In the behavior called stalking the predator reduces the distance as rapidly as possible without stimulating the prey to increase it. When the distance has become short enough, the predator may break into open pursuit, and the prey into open flight. A different sort of interaction follows.
>
> Another example of a social episode is leading and following. This generally arises when two or more individuals are reinforced by a single external system which requires their combined action. . . . The nature of leading and following is clearer when the two kinds of behavior differ considerably and the contingency of reinforcement is complex. A division of labor is usually then required. The leader is primarily under the control of external variables, while the follower is under the control of the leader.[278]

While it is always individuals that behave, the combined behaviors of individuals has given rise to expressions alluding to "group behavior." There are specific variables affect and encourage individuals to conform in a group. One reason is the positive reinforcement associated with joining and conforming within a group. Another substantial reason individuals join and conform within groups is the increased individual power obtained and reinforced by group members. "The reinforcing consequences generated by the group easily exceed the sums of the consequences which could be achieved by the members acting separately. The total reinforcing effect is enormously increased."[279]

These individual and group dynamics are important because as a supervisor you may wonder how what you thought was "one" issue has somehow mushroomed into much more. It is important here to understand that the terms management, motivation, and manipulation as terms in and of themselves are neutral. It is the intent of the individual desirous of changing or influencing the behavior of another that determines whether or not the reinforcing or negative stimulus is abusive or not. Indicators that you, as the administrative authority of your work group, are exerting excessive or inconsistent behavioral reinforcement techniques include:

- Fear. Are you experiencing the oddity that only one or two of your staff really talk to you? Perhaps you've noticed that the rest of your staff only answers the question you have specifically asked. Or, then there's the palpable silence, you rarely ever hear laughter or see people gathering in small groups brainstorming and going "one step" beyond acceptable work expectations.
- Escape. Are you experiencing high turn over? High absenteeism and tardiness? Or, perhaps your staff actually shows up and stays employed but they are lack-luster, withdrawn, and participate in tasks only if it is made mandatory.
- Revolt. Are your administrative superiors typically contacted about "every little thing" you do or want your staff to do? You have to constantly "watch your back" because you know your staff is out to get you? Vandalism is occurring or increasing against personal or office property.
- Passive resistance. You have one or more staff that behaves in just barely acceptable ways, nothing you can reprimand them for, just the person is always a nonconformist.

If you are insensitive (really meaning you are a bully, determinedly difficult, or a predator), you may not even notice these indicators. What you will notice is that you have to: tell everyone exactly what to do, stay on top of staff to get the work product, you just barely meet your bottom—sometimes you do not but there is always a "reason. And then, there is always the quality control issue, your staff always has to be monitored and doubled checked to get things right—but it takes three or four times minimally.

Well, for the sake of fairness, let's just say you are not someone's nemesis; you are just a hard working person who also happens to have the responsibility of supervision as one of your essential job duties. Have you noticed that you have one or more employees who seem to be consuming the majority of your time with appointments in human resources? Do you have an employee who seems to have endless demands for attention, needing to repeatedly explain things, monitor job productivity, keep the peace between co-workers? Do you have an employee that delays productivity because they have to have, in writing, the authorization or law for each and every request you make? Then you, if you did not already know this, have an employee who is your nemesis. And the work world is generally unsympathetic if supervisors "whine" that one or more of their subordinates are bullies, determinedly difficult people or predators. But of course we know they can be, and some are.

The one distinct advantage you have in this particular instance is that you have the administrative authority over this nemesis to affirmatively encourage these employees to modify their behaviors. And, depending on the specifics of their behaviors, productivity, and proficiency you also have some type of progressive disciplinary process that could ultimately lead to the employee's termination. First, consider the following affirmative behavior modification alternatives:

- Be consistent in what is and is not acceptable behavior.
- Never reward or reinforce unacceptable behavior.
- Never infer a behavior, always observe behaviors.
- Let the person know you believe they will follow through on achieving the competent attainment of the essential functions of their job.
- Get verbal confirmation from the employee (or written if on a formal corrective action plan) that they know the appropriate behaviors and work standards.
- Have the employee describe the process that they will use to accomplish their behavior modification and/or the accomplishment of their job.
- Acknowledge you are counting on them to achieve, with excellence the modified behavior and/or the work.
- Acknowledge their accomplishments in a way that is appreciated by the employee.

AFFIRMATIVE DEFENSES TO BULLIES, DIFFICULT PEOPLE, AND PREDATORS AS SUPERVISORS

Have you noticed that you are working in a an atmosphere where there is abusive anger, accusing and blaming, judging and criticizing, withholding, perhaps even denial that things happened? Have you noticed that your work accomplishments and contributions have been "dammed with too faint praise"? That your requests for explanations about work procedures, processes, and inclusion in team projects are met with non-commitment and evasive posturing? If you have, then you probably have noticed that your self-perception is increasingly disintegrating and you are second guessing yourself more than ever. You feel as though you are perpetually "on guard" and your distrust of those in your work environment continually increases.

Supervisors and others who are in your administrative chain of command have tremendous power in your work life, but then you already know this. Of course individual personalities, work cultures, and customer demands for your businesses product or service influence your supervisor's behavior when under stress. But one skill, your ability to pay attention to your supervisor's management style and priorities, in the long run will be extremely beneficial. Some of us based on any number of reasons have come to the conclusion that coaching, mentoring, modeling, and manipulating your supervisor falls at either one or the other extreme: "kissing up" or bulling. In truth, every successful interaction and relationship contains elements of coaching, mentoring, modeling, and manipulating, intent is intrinsic to one's motive. Your action alone will not ensure avoidance or evasion of all unwanted disparate treatment. However, your accurate assessment of your immediate supervisor's leadership style may prevent or mitigate her becoming your nemesis, see the following Tables 9 and 10.

First you need to correctly assess how much personal interaction (relationship orientation) you typically need. Then you need to determine how much personal interaction you typically have with your immediate supervisor. You might also want to see if this interaction is constant with others that she supervises. If you are not being treated differently in terms of the personal interaction, then you need to determine what type of leadership style your supervisor most frequently displays. You may even want to consider what type of leadership style your supervisor displays when she's under pressure. Finally you will want to determine how production driven she is. The degree of tension between the two of you increases the more the two of you are different in each of these areas. A hint, experiment for one week and mimic your supervisor's relationship orientation, leadership style, and task orientation. At the end of the week see if things didn't seem to go just a bit more smoothly. If you were subtle about your mirroring your supervisor she didn't even get suspicious about what you were doing. If you keep this up, you will be the new "star" employee for your supervisor.

Table 9. Blake and Mouton (1964), Managers Typed by Their Leadership Style

Type of Leadership Style	Relationship Orientation	Task Orientation
• Tough-minded, no-nonsense production prodder	• Extremely low	• Extremely high
• Country-club leader	• Extremely high	• Extremely low
• Laissez-faire, abdicator of responsibility	• Extremely low	• Extremely low
• Compromiser	• Moderate	• Moderate
• Integrator of task accomplishment with trust and commitment from followers	• Extremely high	• Extremely high

Table 10.   Blake and Mouton's Manager's Style Typed by Low/High Consequences

Type of Leadership	Relationship Orientation	Task Orientation	Effectiveness
• Deserter	• Low	• Low	• Low
• Autocrat	• Low	• High	• Low
• Missionary	• High	• Low	• Low
• Compromiser	• High	• High	• Low
• Bureaucrat	• Low	• Low	• High
• Benevolent autocrat	• Low	• High	• High
• Developer	• High	• Low	• High
• Executive	• High	• High	• High

FROM QUANTUM LEAPS TO STRINGS: DEALING WITH PEOPLE IS ALL ABOUT PERCEPTIONS

Can you imagine a working in an environment where everything you want to know is immediately accessible to you? Can you imagine working in an environment where internal "office politics" is a moot concern? Can you imagine never needing a performance review because your performance, at all times is known to everyone you work with, and of course you know the same about your co-workers and chain of command? Can you imagine never again having to endure verbal abuse or any type of mistreatment from a bully, determinedly difficult person, or predator? Well, whether or not you can imagine this and more—start practicing—because we are standing at the threshold of this being the norm. In fact, some of the people you now know are accessing this type of information at work right now, regularly, thus their apparent detached, nonchalant attitude. How? Just suppose there is something to this "interconnected consciousness" stuff touted by Quantum Physics, String Theory, and related interpersonal sensory perception studies. As an example, a basic review of the newest consideration, String Theory's business interpersonal relationship application might be worth considering—lets just say for the sake of conversation.

String theory, which has the potential to interweave all of nature's forces and material constituents within a single theoretical tapestry[280]—really does have practical application for ordinary folks like you and me. The features of string theory require that we drastically change our understanding of space, time, and matter, all of which can be excruciating (for some of us at some time) at work.

Warping our belief system around the possibility that each of us has the ability—right now—to change "the reality" at work, for some of us may take time to comprehend. For some of us to "get used to" the idea that our intent creates our reality can unbelievable. So, for some of us to allow the possibility that our voice is energy which manifests our last intent, to sink into our belief systems and values at a comfortable level might just be inconceivable.

So, if this concept is an impossibility, how about just thinking about the last time you had some goal you just had to achieve. You know, when you saved to buy your house, or for school, or something else that you were willing to place as your first priority and you focused on obtaining. For you during this time of intense focus, dedication, and perhaps sacrifice were there periods where you just seemed to "loose track of time"? Well, if this has ever happened to you, you've glimpsed one aspect of String Theory.

For, in String Theory, space and time, can no longer to be thought of as an inert backdrop left to scientist, science fiction writers, and anyone else but you. String Theory requires its own severe revamping of our conceptions of space and time—our conscious awareness has been "tickled" will we, you and I, respond? String Theory is "the next step" after Quantum Theory, and supports our current understanding of quantum consciousness. But until each of us embrace the possibilities, incorporating the power of our ability to: manifest form, to change reality, to influence others; we will continue to operate under paradigms of power submission. Personally making the transition, considering the possibility that your beliefs and values might expand to include something new might be viewed as similar to your accepting the computer technological revolution. Some us will never touch a computer, some will but only if they have to, some will and gain various degrees of proficiency. And some of us not only can use computers we can build them, repair them, write programs for them—and envision the next generation of wireless information storage, exchange, and manipulation.

If space, substance, and time in this new paradigm operate differently then so to does your ability to access information from any source. If space, substance, and time are continuously accessible to you then office secretes, subversive cliques, devious antics of bullies, determinedly difficult people, and predators are known to you. If you are aware then you are no longer "the prey." Interesting concept . . . Hum? However, until all of us reach this level of constant, open communication at work, let us look at the alternatives of dealing with your work nemesis.

Simply put, if words and/or behaviors of another dis-empower, disrespect, or devalue you, that person is being abusive to you. When you are ready, willing, and able to commit to changing your work environment—and not before—you will commit the necessary energy and action to change your situation. When your awareness expands to include the interconnectivity of consciousness you will permanently neutralize bullies, determinedly difficult people, and predators. Voice is energy, energy creates form.

NOTES

276. Skinner, Burrhus F., *Science and Human Behavior*. (Free Press: New York, 1965), 299.

277. Skinner, Science and Human, 303.

278. Skinner, Science and Human, 304–305.

279. Skinner, Science and Human, 312.

280. Green, Brian, The Elegant Universe: Superstrings, Hidden Dimensions, And the Quest for The Ultimate Theory. (W.W. Norton: New York, 2003).

Chapter Nine

Transformational Leadership and Consciousness

Transformation is an awakening. When the awakening comes in you, when you finally say wait a minute I wonder what the real purpose in life is . . . what happens when you ask that question? What happens is . . . at the moment that you decided to follow you're Voice, to follow your interior, in that instant you go through a reversal. You go from living life in which matter is more important than your inner world to recognizing the inner world is more important than the external world. This is Transformation, this is it—where you reverse yourself, you go from living a life in which you see the outside world coming toward you—and then you realize that wait, your inside world comes first; and it shapes and it forms the outside world. When this (awakening) finally drops down into your being everything is different.

Caroline Myss

There is increasing spiritual, scientific, and psychological research supporting the long-standing proverbs that our intentions (voice) both manifest and attract your energetic output.[281] With few exceptions, where you work and with whom you work is the result of your personal choice. If you voluntarily decided to compete for your job, it was after you made an infinite number of personal choices related to education, prior experiences, geographic location, and entanglements with family and friends. So this job is what you "asked for." No, you did not ask to work in a hostile work environment, but you have not quit. And yes, there will always be some compelling reason to keep working (pay, prestige, autonomy—whatever) until you reach the critical point of "not one moment more at this place." Do not be hard on yourself, your staying or leaving your current work situation is neither "good" nor "bad"—it just "is." Like all other jobs at some time you may have your share of annoyances, bullies, determinedly difficult people, and predators close at hand. Chapter 8 reviewed some practical steps to deflect, neutralize, or stop being verbally abused, harassed, and discriminated against. But these "solutions" are only a superficial "fix" which will need "tweaking" as time changes and so does the "face" of your nemesis. The only way of permanently neutralize all nemesis' at work—but better yet—to excel and profit at work is through authentic self-assessment and conscious awareness: in other words knowing your religious/spiritual/consciousness values and "walking your talk."

IT MAY NOT BE FAIR, BUT YOU HAVE TO CHANGE FIRST

As you realize the correlation between work, money, survival, and prestige internal tension often forms. Much of this tension, if it exists, is the result of your internal conflict between your core values, issues of survival, acquaintance with balancing personal power, and submissiveness. These concerns, if strong enough develop into fears, and these fears consciously or not often exert a powerful control on your reactions and the direction your life takes. In order to learn about your motives, your intentions, your reactions, you need to form relationships.

Relationships, particularly those at work often generate conflict, conflict generates choice, choice generates movement, and movement generates more conflict.[282] The only way to permanently break free of this vicious cycle is to be aware that you are—interconnected with and a part of—everything else. So, when dealing with your nemesis remember that when you do something different your nemesis must also do something different. When you remove the "reward and satisfaction" your nemesis achieves he will stop his behavior. Yes, he will be irritated and need to have this "new" behavior reinforced. However, his actions toward you either satisfies some need, or gives him pleasure. The fascinating and transforming revelation occurs when you realize that because you are interconnected with your nemesis, if and when you change—even just a little—your nemesis will have to respond to you differently! (OK, he's responding to the law suit you just won but that is a new and different response from you.)

Once your awareness changes, your intentions change, then your actions change, and then invariably your work life: associations, productivity, effectiveness, and income change. Conscious awareness breaks you out of habitual patterns of behavior, thoughts, and relationships. Heightened awareness sensitizes you to the abundance of synchronistic opportunities and serendipitous pleasures that tickle your senses and fertilize your visions and our voice. Sometimes, the tangible manifestations of affirming occurrences scare you, trigger low self-esteem, or feed your skepticism. The abundant manifestations of your hopes, dreams, and wishes may be incomprehensible or perhaps you just do not feel deserving.

How do you, (for each of us has our repressed vulnerabilities); transcend habits, fears, and in some instances social conditioning to attract abundance and protect yourself from those pesky "nemesis" at work? The first discipline to be practiced is one of detachment. But, how do you practicably apply detachment? Becoming detached and conscious means sorting through your "established" perceptions regarding how you "should" or "must" respond to people and situations. It means identifying those perceptions you have that are religious/spiritual "Truths" and living them so that their energy is yours. A spiritual "Truth" has the optimum, affirmative benefit for all as the outcome.[283]

The ability to release the hurt, anger, and often-sick feeling you get from exposure to your nemesis is not easy. At first your major accomplishment may be a few moments at work without pain, worry, resentment, or hostility. When you catch yourself in one of these fleeting moments of peace and/or balance at work, freeze this feeling. Savor this feeling, and start getting use to this feeling at work. This feeling of "relief," quiet, at oneness in chaos, transcends any bedevilment perpetuated towards you by your nemesis. This "detachment" is what is meant by living in the present moment. The more you live in the present moment the more you live in the present moment. But how can you be detached when you know for a fact that you are surrounded by an assortment of individuals who have their self interest, promotions, and profit at heart?

The detachment part is that you may be quite aware of what torment your nemesis has heaped upon you, but you are detached because you do not react, because you are beyond worrying about your "safety." The "peace" in detachment comes from knowing that no one person or group of people can determine your life's path.[284] Now, depending on what is occurring, you will be accurately documenting, and taking appropriate steps with your civil rights officer, equal opportunity officer, human resource manager, labor representative, or legal counsel if the situation warrants. However, inclusive of specific defensive legal action, you must remember that living fully "in this present moment," means knowing that no situation or person will be exactly the same tomorrow, everything changes. Your nemesis may in fact escalate her aggressive behavior toward you for a bit (told you they would change) but the more outrageous her behavior, the sooner she will have to stop. Why? Because now her behavior is in the open, is being addressed and let's face it your employer is more interested in saving money than supporting your nemesis. Nemesis who act outside the scope of their employment while representing their employer cost the employer big money, and often themselves personally. Also, if your nemesis's mistreatment of you was once sanctioned by others as the mistreatment escalates others become more and more uncomfortable. The backlash toward your nemesis will increase so that her offensive behavior will stop or she will leave.

It may take some time for your nemesis to stop so this is where your discipline and commitment to your values are forged. You will not go through this alone; you and your support team, your values (the best possible outcome for all) will in fact manifest just that. How long will it take for the manifestation to occur: as long as it takes. So, throw away your clocks, calendars, and become acutely aware. Live in "this" moment realizing that you have a hundred percent possibilities—a hundred percent of the time—until you make a choice. Life is unfolding as it should. See what happens and how powerful you are when you make the first move.

LEVELS OF LEADERSHIP CONSCIOUSNESS, YOURS

Regardless of your current state of conscious awareness, you are someplace on the continuum. Know this. Your placement on the consciousness continuum is irrelevant, the fact that you are, at some level already consciously aware is what is important. This is an important realization and confirmation because now that you know this, you can never completely deny your inclusion. This also means that your awareness evolution is constant, uninterrupted, and continuous. This means that once you conceive a possibility, a vision, voice your intent, you will act upon this, the time it takes for you to act and your intent to materialize is inconsequential because you manifest when it is time. Well, you say, enough of the double talk, what does this mean?

Well, first take a look at fear, any fear you may have and choose to ponder at this moment. The power of fear is the anticipation that an undesirable consequence will happen. If you have not considered this before, realize that no consequence you may experience will affect only you. Now, at the moment this may not make you feel any better, but follow this thought through. Even if your consequence has negative, let's say horrific consequences on someone you care about, you must realize that when you and at least one other person's consciousness has the same intent based in "Truth" (the optimum benefit for all involved) the outcome is perfect for you. Yes, you'll need your self-discipline not to "give up" five minutes before the "miracle"—but a "miracles" always manifest from your Truth's intent. Once you change your thinking you discover people are your greatest resource and you theirs. This awareness increases your personal power which in turn execrates your successfulness.

Your perceptions, stemming from your core values, socialization, and desires, influence each and every one of your decisions. Your ability to trust your "knowingness" from your quieted center gives you the power to relax in the chaos of work emerging as part of the beautiful tapestry your work contributes to yourself and your community. If your work was not important and contributed to the overall benefit of your community, you would not have a job. Sometimes your being in a particular job, at a particular time, working with specific people is not about your benefit. You just might be where you are, doing what you do, because you will or have benefited someone else. You never really know the impact you have on someone else and that casual word of support, that helpful service, that answered phone might be decisive in someone else's life.

Simply put, you will see what you are willing and able to see. You will always move toward your values and away from what threatens your values. And, you may be in a particular place, doing a certain thing, at a specific time for someone else's benefit, not yours. So quit whining because what you focus on will be drawn to you, even if it is something you say you don't want—you are still focusing on it. In other words, the miracle didn't happen if you didn't see it. What have you done lately to contribute to your healthy work environment?

DEDICATED TO THE READER: QUIET FIRE

Sometimes the way one retains new information best it to practice using this information immediately and often. Sometimes, new information is engrained in us by physically doing something that we can associate in a positive way with the new information. Sometimes, replaying so that we can "re-hear" the information over and over again in our minds cements the desired information for instant retrieval when necessary.

The transformational leadership and proactive management principles discussed in relationship to neutralizing bullies, determinedly difficult people and predators at work will resonate differently with each of you. Your individual needs, level of conscious awareness, and the significance your work plays in your life will determine what, and how much of this work you will apply in your work relationships. The point is, once something has been read, it can not be "unread." So, on some level, throughout time some part of this information will be available when needed because you read it. In preparing this book for your reading, you have been envisioned as a small, quiet fire. Depending on your vision, voice, situation, needs, and satisfaction saturation level you will fend off bullies, determinedly difficult people, and predators based on your energy level and "burning desires" (values). More importantly, each of you at some time will lead either formally or informally your co-workers, administrative superiors, customers, and various other stakeholders. Until you ignite, fully utilizing the energetic power of your voice, you are a quiet fire. Therefore, following metaphor is dedicated to you as you smolder, awaiting to ignite.

Quiet Fire
Often "ordinary" people with quiet concerns are discounted, overlooked or even purposefully censored. Sometimes being "quiet" is seen as:

- being unobtrusive, not Being;
- being still, not being observant;
- being predictable, not awaiting opportunity;
- being motionless, not developing strategy;
- being calm, not sensual tingling with anticipation.

Often the "leader" is not the most obvious, popular, infamous, famous, or even wealthiest individual in the "group'. Like fire, a leader has:

- the tendency, innately, to be taken for granted as a natural phenomenon;
- a long kindling ability until fully ignited by, poverty, injustice, civil need, war, social transition, organizational reconstruction or moral indignation;
- funding if there is a "power" base:
- power if "fueled" by a cause and supporters cause and effect which may be benevolent or malicious, depending on one's perspective and values;
- intensity, which usually escalates over time;
- the potential to have unanticipated consequences, and
- clears, disinfects, and provides for new beginnings.

Awareness precedes appearance. Awareness is one's Voice—which creates form. "Quiet Fires" are the Leadership Voices™ that consciously ignite interaction and group dynamics, which produce exemplary, profitable products and services. Voice is energy, energy creates form.

NOTES

284. Greene, Brian, The Elegant Universe: Superstrings, Hidden Dimensions, And the Quest for The Ultimate Theory. (W.W. Norton: New York, 2003). Herbert, Nick, Quantum Reality: Beyond the New Physics an Excursion into Metaphysics and The Meaning of Reality. (Anchor Books, Doubleday: New York, 1985). Nick, Quantum Reality: Beyond the New Physics an Excursion into Metaphysics and The Meaning of Reality. (Anchor Books, Doubleday: New York, 1985). Irby , Linda, Leadership Voices™: Values, Proactive Management, and Consciousness. (UMI: 304 1369, 2002). Mapes, James. J., Quantum Leap Thinking: An Owner's Guide to the Mind. Dove Books: Beverly Hills, 1996). McTaggart, Lynne, The Field: The Quest for the Secret Force of the Universe. (HarperCollins: New York, 2002). Myss, Carolyn.

(1996). Anatomy of the Spirit: The Seven Stages of Power and Healing. Harmony Books: New York. Carolyn, Sacred Contracts: Awakening Your Divine Potential. (Sounds True: Boulder CO, 2001). Wheatley, , Margaret J, Leadership and The New Science: Learning About Organization from an Orderly Universe. (Berrett-Koehler: San Francisco, 1992). Wheatley, Margaret. J. and Myron Kellner-Rogers, A Simpler Way. (Berrett-Koehler: San Francisco, 1996). Wolinsky, Wolinsky, Stephen, *Quantum Consciousness: The Guide to Experiencing Quantum Psychology.* (Bramble Books: Northfork, Conn.,1993). Wolinsky, Stephen, *The Way of The Human: Volume I Developing Multi-Dimensional Awareness. The Quantum Psychology Notebooks* (Special section: Trances people live revised). (Quantum Institute: Capitola, Cali. 1999a). Wolinsky, Stephen, *The Way Of The Human: Volume II The False Core And The False Self. The Quantum Psychology Notebooks.* (Quantum Institute: Capitola, California, 1999b). Wolinsky, Stephen, *The Way Of The Human: Volume III Beyond Quantum Psychology: The Quantum Psychology Notebooks.* (Special section: Trances people live revised) (Quantum Institute: Capitola, California, 1999c).

282. Myss, Anatomy, 135.

283. Capri, Fritjof, The Web of Life: A New Scientific Understanding of Living Systems. (Doubleday: New York, 1996). Chopra, Deepak, The Higher Self. (Simon and Schuster: New York, 1993). Chopra, Deepak, The Seven Spiritual Laws of Success: A Practical Guide to the Fulfillment of Your Dreams. (Amber-Allen Publishing: San Rafael, Cal., 1994). Greene, Brian, *The Elegant Universe: Superstrings, Hidden Dimensions, And the Quest for The Ultimate Theory.* (W.W. Norton: New York, 2003). Greenleaf, Robert. K., *Servant Leadership: A Journey into the Nature of Legitimate Power and Greatness.* (Paulist Press: New York, 1982). Myss, Carolyn. (1996). *Anatomy Of The Spirit: The Seven Stages of Power and Healing.* Harmony Books: New York.

284. Myss, Anatomy, 242.

Bibliography

1993 Parliament of Religions-Chicago. *Our Religions: The Seven World Religions Introduced By Preeminent Scholars from Each Tradition.* Arvind Sharma (Ed.) Harper: San Francisco.

Alder, Ronald B. and Neil Towne. (1993). *Looking Out/Looking In* (7th ed.). Harcourt Brace Jovanovich College Publishers: Fla.

Argyle, Michael. (1974). *The Social Psychology of Work*, (Penguin Books: Wrights Lane, London.

Autry, James A. (1991). *Love and Profit: The Art of Caring Leadership.* Avon Press: New York.

Aziz, Robert. (1990). *C.G. Jung's Psychology of Religion and Synchronicity.* State University of New York Press.

Baldwin, Martha. (1987). *Self-Sabotage: How to Stop it and Soar to Success.* Warner Books: New York.

Bass, Bernard M. (1990). *Bass and Stogdill's Handbook of Leadership: Theory, Research and Managerial Applications.* The Free Press: New York.

Beauchamp, Tom L. and Norman E. Bowie. (1988). *Ethical Theory and Business.* (Third Edition) Prentice Hall: New Jersey.

Beckhard, Richard, and Wendy Pritchard. (1992). *Changing the Essence: The Art Of Creating and Leading Fundamental Changes in Organizations.* Jossey-Bass Publishers: San Francisco.

Bellah, Robert N. et al. (1985). *Habits of the Heart: Individualism and Commitment in American Life.* Harper and Row: New York.

Bellah, Robert N. et al. (1991). *The Good Society.* Alfred A. Knopf: New York.

Bennis, Warren and Burt Nanus. (1985). *Leaders: The Strategies for Taking Charge.* Harper and Row: New York.

Bennis, Warren G. (1989). *On Becoming A Leader.* Addison-Wesley: Menlo Park.

Bernstein, Albert J. (2001). *Emotional Vampires: Dealing with People Who Drain You Dry.* McGraw-Hill: New York.

Bernstein, Albert J. and Sydney C. Rozen. (1992). *Neanderthals at Work: How People and Politics Can Drive You Crazy. And What You Can Do About Them*. Ballantine Books: New York.

Billingsley, Andrew. (1968). *Black Families in White America*. Simon and Schuster Inc.: New York.

Blake, Robert R. et al. (1964). Breakthrough in Organization Development. *Harvard Business Review*, *42*, 133–135.

Bolman, Lee G. and Terrence E. Deal. (1991). *Reframing Organizations: Artistry, Choice, and Leadership*. Jossey-Bass: San Francisco.

Bolman, Lee. G. et. al. (1995). *Leading With Soul: An Uncommon Journey Of Spirit*. Jossey-Bass: San Francisco.

Bolton, Robert, and Dorothy Grover Bolton. (1996). *People Styles at Work: Making Bad Relationships Good and Good Relationships Better*. American Management Association: New York.

Bouwsma, William J. (1988). *John Calvin: A Sixteenth Century Portrait*. Oxford University Press: New York.

Bridges, William. (1991). *Managing Transitions: Making the Most Of Change*. Addison-Wesley: Massachusetts.

Bridges, William. (1994). *Job Shift*. Addison-Wesley: New York.

Bucke, Richard M. (1923). *Cosmic Consciousness: A Study in The Evolution of The Human Mind*. Penguin Books: New York.

Burns James M. (1978). *Leadership*. Harper and Row: New York.

Campbell, Susan M. (1984). *Beyond the Power Struggle*. Impact: San Luis Obispo, Calif.

Capri, Fritjof. (1996). *The Web of Life: A New Scientific Understanding of Living Systems*. Doubleday: New York.

Carter, Jay. (1989). *How to Stop Being Hurt by them Without Becoming One of Them*. Barnes and Noble. Inc.: New York.

Chopra, Deepak. (1993). *The Higher Self*. Simon and Schuster: New York.

Chopra, Deepak. (1994). *The Seven Spiritual Laws of Success: A Practical Guide to the Fulfillment of Your Dreams*. Amber-Allen Publishing: San Rafael, Calif.

Cohen, Herb. (1993). *New Perspectives On Negotiating*. Harper Collins Publisher, Inc.: New York.

Compilation (A Harvard Business Review Book), (1992). Leaders on Leadership: Interviews with Top Executives. Preference by Warren Bennis.

Covey, Steven R. (1989). *The 7 Habits of Highly Effective People*. Simon and Schuster: New York.

Covey, Steven R. (1992). *Principled Centered Leadership: Give A Man A Fish and You Feed Him For A Day; Teach Him How To Fish And You Feed Him For A Lifetime*. Simon and Schuster: New York.

Cox Taylor. (1993). *Cultural Diversity in Organizations: Theory, Research, And Practice*. Berrett-Koehler Publisher: San Francisco.

Davison, Gerald D. and John M. Neil. (1990). *Abnormal Psychology: Fifth Edition*. John Wiley and Sons: New York.

Deming, W. Edward. (1986). *Drastic Changes for Western Management*. Center for Quality and Productivity Improvement: Madison, Wis.

Deming, W. Edward. (1986b). *Out Of The Crisis*. Massachusetts Institute of Technology, Center for Advanced Engineering Study: Cambridge, Mass.

Deming, W. Edward. (1991). *Deming's 14 Points Applied to Services*. Marcel Dekker, Inc.: New York.

DePree, Max. (1989). *Leadership Is An Art*. Dell Trade: New York.

DePree, Max. (1992). *Leadership Jazz*. Doubleday: New York.

Deutsche, David. (1998). *The Fabric of Reality: The Science of Parallel Universes and Its Implication*. Viking Penguin: New York.

Dickson, John A. (1973). *New Analytical Bible and Dictionary of the Bible*. Authorized King James Version with comprehensive general index edition. John A. Dickinson Publishing Co.: Chicago.

Dilenschneider, Robert. L. (1990). *Power and Influence: Mastering the Art of Persuasion*. Prentice Hall Press: New York.

Donaldson-Pressman, Stephanie. and Robert Pressman. (1994). *The Narcissistic Family: Diagnosis and Treatment*. Jossey-Bass: San Francisco.

Dorsey, David (1994). *The Force*. Random House: New York.

Doyle, William, and William Perkins. (1994). *Smash the Pyramid: 100 Career Secrets From America's Fastest-Rising Executives*. Warner Books: New York.

Dreamer, Orah M. (1999). *The Invitation*. Harper Collins: San Francisco.

Drucker, Peter F. (1967). *The Effective Executive*. Harper and Row: San Francisco.

Ebenstein, William. (1969). *Great Political Thinkers: Plato to the Present*. (Fourth edition). Holt, Rinehart and Winston, Inc.: New York.

Edelman, Joel and M. B. Crain. (1993). *The Tao Of Negotiation: How You Can Prevent, Resolve And Transcend Conflict In Work And Everyday Life*. Harper Business: New York.

Effler, William B. (1994). *Leadership By God's Design: Spirituality For Leadership's Personal And Corporate Growth*. DIA, 55(6A) 1600.

Eisler, Riane. (1987). *The Chalice and The Blade: Our History, Our Future*. Harper: San Francisco.

Elgin, Suzette H. (1997). *How to Turn the Other Cheek and Still Survive in Today's World*. Thomas Nelson Publishers: Nashville.

English, Harace B, and Ava C. English. (1966). *A Comprehensive Dictionary of Psychological And Psychoanalytical Terms. A Guide to Usage, for Readers and Writers in the Fields of Psychology, Psychoanalysis, Psychiatry, Education, Guidance, and Social Work*. David McKay Company, Inc.: New York.

Evans, Patricia. (1992). *The Verbally Abusive Relationship: How to Recognize It and How To Respond*. Bob Adams, Inc.: Holbrook, Massachusetts.

Evans, Patricia. (1993). *Verbal Abuse Survivors Speak Out: On Relationship and Recovery*. Bob Adams, Inc. Holbrook, Mass.

Evans, Patricia. (2002). *Controlling People: How to Recognize, Understand, and Deal with People Who Try to Control You*. Adams Media Corporation: Avon, Mass.

Farson, Richard. (1996). *Management of the Absurd: Paradoxes in Leadership*. Simon and Schuster: New York.

Fisher, Roger, and William Ury. (1981). *Getting To Yes: Negotiating Agreement Without Giving In*. (Second edition). Penguin Books: New York.

Bibliography

Forbes, Beverly A. (1991). *Profile Of The Leader Of The Future: Origin, Premises, Values And Characteristics Of The Theory F Transformational Leadership Model.* Unpublished manuscript. Seattle, Wash., October 1993.

Ford, Leighton. (1991). *Transforming Leadership: Jesus' Way of Creating Vision, Shaping Values and Empowering Change.* InterVarsity Press: Downers Grove, Ill.

Forward, Susan. (1997). *Emotional Blackmail: When the People in Your Life Use Fear, Obligation, and Guilt to Manipulate You.* Harper-Collins Publishers: New York.

Fruehling, Rosemary. T. and Joan M. Lacombe. (1966). *Communicating for Results.* EMC Paradigm: St Paul, Minn.

Gardiner, John. J. (1988). Building leadership teams. In M.F. Green (Ed.) *Leaders for A New Era: Strategies for Higher Education.* (pp. 137–153). American Council on Education/ MacMillan Publishing: New York.

Gardiner, John. J. (1993). *Beyond Leader and Community: Creating New Metaphors Of Governance For American Higher Education.* Article. Seattle, Wash.

Gardiner, John. J. and Beverly A. Forbes. *Preparing Effective Leaders For An Interdependent World: Seattle University's Multidisciplinary Doctoral Cohorts.* Paper presented to the National Leadership Group of the American Council on Education, Washington, D.C. December 3, 1993.

Gardner, John W. (1990). *On Leadership.* The Free Press: New York.

Gilbreath, Robert D. (1993). *Escape From Management Hell: 12 Tales of Horror, Humor, And Heroism.* Berrett-Koehler Publishers: San Francisco.

Gillespie, Richard C. (1992). *Managing Is Everybody's Business.* Work/Life Books: Everett, WA.

Gilligan, Carol. (1993). *In A Different Voice: Psychological Theory and Women's Development.* Harvard University Press: Cambridge.

Gleick, James. (1987). *Chaos: Making A New Science.* Penguin Books: New York.

Goleman, Daniel. (1995). *Emotional Intelligence: Why It Can Matter More Than IQ.* Bantam Books: New York.

Greene, Brian. (2003). *The Elegant Universe: Superstrings, Hidden Dimensions, And the Quest for The Ultimate Theory.* W.W. Norton: New York.

Greenleaf, Robert. K. (1982). *Servant Leadership: A Journey into the Nature of Legitimate Power and Greatness.* Paulist Press: New York.

Gretz, Karl. F. and Steven R. Drozdeck. (1992) *Empowering Innovative People.* Prous Publishing Company: Chicago.

Grim, Patrick. (2005). *Questions of Value.* The Teaching Company: Chantilly, VA.

Gwaltney, John L. (1981). *Drylongso: A Self-Portrait of Black America.* Vintage Books: New York.

Hall, Brian P. and Helen Thompson. (1980). *Leadership Through Values.* Paulist Press: New York.

Hammond, Joshua and James Morrison. (1996), *Stuff Americans Are Made Of: Seven Cultural Forces That Define Americans—A New Framework for Quality, Productivity and Profitability.* Simon and Schuster Macmillan Company: New York.

Hare, Robert D. (1993). *Without Conscience: The Disturbing World of the Psychopaths among Us.* Gilford Press: New York.

Harris, W. Lee. (1990). *Effective Church Leadership: A Practical Sourcebook.* Augsburg Fortress: Minn.

Heider, John. (1985). *The Tao of Leadership: Leadership Strategies for A New Age.* Bantam Books: New York.

Helmstetter, Shad. (1987). *The Self-Talk Solution: Take Control of Your Life-With the Self-Management Program for Success.* Pocket Books: New York.

Herbert, Nick. (1985). *Quantum Reality: Beyond the New Physics an Excursion into Metaphysics and The Meaning of Reality.* Anchor Books, Doubleday: New York.

Herbert, Nick. (1993). *Elemental Mind: Human Consciousness and The New Physics.* Plume: New York.

Hersey, Paul. and Kenneth H. Blanchard. (1977). *Management of Organizational Behavior: Utilizing Human Resources.* Prentice-Hall: Englewood Cliffs.

Hess, Beth B., Elizeabeth W. Markson, and Peter J. Stein. (1988). *Sociology: Third Edition.* MacMillan Publishing Company: New York.

Hitt, William D. (1990). *Ethics and Leadership: Putting Theory into Practice.* Battelle Press: Columbus, Ohio.

Hogan, Robert, et al. (1997). *Handbook of Personality Psychology.* Academic Press: San Diego.

Hogan, Robert, and Robert B. Kaiser. (2004). "What We Know About Leadership."

Hogan, Robert, and Robert B. Kaiser. (2005). "The Dark Side of Discretion: Leader Personality and Organizational Ineffectiveness." In preparation for J. Antonakis and R. Hooijberg (Eds.) *Leadership In and of Organizations, July 2005.*

Hollander, Edwin. P. (1978). *Leadership Dynamics: A Practical Guide to Effective Relationships.* The Free Press: New York.

Holroyd, Stuart. (1977). *PSI and the Consciousness Explosion.* Taplinger: New York.

Irby, Linda. (2002) Leadership Voices™: Values, Proactive Management, and Consciousness. *UMI: 304 1369.*

Jacobsen, Stephen E. (1994). *Spirituality and Leadership in Secular Settings: A Delhi Study.* Seattle University.

James, Jennifer. (1987). *Windows.* Expanded edition. Newmarket Press: New York.

James, Jennifer. (1990). *You Know I Wouldn't Say This If I Didn't Love You: How To Defend Yourself Against Verbal Zaps And Zingers.* Revised, expanded edition of *The Slug Manual: The Rise and Fall of Criticism.* Newmarket Press: New York.

James, Jennifer. (1996). *Thinking in the Future Tense: Leadership Skills for a New Age.* Simon and Schuster: New York.

Jamieson, David, and Julie O'Mara. (1991). *Managing Workforce 2000: Gaining the Diversity Advantage.* Forward by Warren Bennis. Jossey-Bass: San Francisco.

Jaworski, Joseph. (1996). *Synchronicity : The Inner Path Of Leadership.* Berrett-Koehler Inc.: San Francisco.

Johansen, Robert and Rob Swigart. (1994). *Upsizing the Individual In The Downsized Organization: Managing in The Wake Of Reengineering, Globalization, And Overwhelming Technological Change.* Doddison-Wesley Publishing: New York.

Jung, Carl. G. (1969). *The Psychological Foundations of Belief in Spirits and The Soul and Death.* Extracted from Volume 8, *The Structure and Dynamics of the Psyche* (2nd ed.). Princeton University Press.

Jung, Carl. G. (1973). *Synchronicity: An Acausal Connecting Principle*. Translation by R. F. C. Hull. From the Collected Works of C. G. Jung, Volume 8. Bollingen Series: Princeton University Press.

Jung, Carl. G. (1977). *Psychology and the Occult*. Translation by R. F. C. Hull. From the Collected Works of C. G. Jung, Volumes 1, 8, and 18. Bollingen Series: Princeton University Press.

Jung, Carl. G. (1990). *The Undiscovered Self: With Symbols and the Interpretation of Dreams*. In the Revised Translation by R. F. C. Hull with a new introduction by W. McGuire. From Volume 10 of the Collected Works of C. G. Jung, *Civilization in Transition* (Second Edition). Bollingen Series: Princeton University Press.

Keirsey, David and Marilyn Bates. (1984). *Please Understand Me: Character and Temperament Types*. Prometheus Nemesis: Del Mar, Calif.

Kersting, Karen. "Turning Happiness into Economic Power: Positive Psychology Summit Speakers Discussed the Benefits of a Contented Society." *Monitor on Psychology*. Volume 34, No. 11 December 2003.

Kotex, John. P. (1995). *The New Rules: How To Succeed In Today's Post-Corporate World*. The Free Press: New York.

Kouzes, James. M. and Barry Z. Posner. (1987). *The Leadership Challenge: How To Get Extraordinary Things Done in Organizations*. San Francisco: Jossey-Bass.

Kouzes, James. M. and Barry Z. Posner. (1993). *Credibility: How Leaders Gain And Lose It, Why People Demand It*. Jossey-Bass: San Francisco.

Kreitner, Robert and Angelo Kinicki. (1992). *Organizational Behavior*. Irwin: Homewood, IL.

Lawler, Edward, et al. (1980). *Organizational Assessment, Perspectives on the Measurement of Organizational Behavior and the Quality of Work Life*. John Wiley and Sons: New York.

Lens, Sidney. (1973). *The Labor Wars: From the Molly Maguries to the Sit-Downs*. Doubleday and Company, Inc.: New York.

Lerner, Harriet. (1993). *The Dance of Deception: A Guide to Authenticity and Truth-Telling In Women's Relationships*. Harper-Collins Publishers: New York.

Lipton, Bruce. (2005). *Biology of Belief: Unleashing the Power of Consciousness, Matter, and Miracles*. Mountain of Love/Elite Books: Santa Rosa, Calif.

Locke, Ewin A., et al. (1991). *The Essence of Leadership: The Four Keys to Leading Successfully*. Lexington Books: New York.

Machiavelli, Nicco. (1981). *The Prince*. Translated with an introduction by George Bull. Penguin Books: New York.

Mapes, James. J. (1996). *Quantum Leap Thinking: An Owner's Guide to the Mind*. Dove Books: Beverly Hills.

Marinoble, R. M. (1990). *Faith and Leadership: The Spiritual Journeys of Transformational Leaders*. Doctoral Dissertation, The University of San Diego, 1990.

Martin, Joanne and Debra Meyerson.(1988). *Organizational Cultures and The Denial, Channeling and Acknowledgment of Ambiguity*. In L. R. Pondy, R. J. Boland, Jr. and H. Thomas (Eds.), *Managing Ambiguity and Change*. (pp. 93–126). John Wiley and Sons: New York.

Mason, Paul T. and Randi Kreger. (1998), *Stop Walking on Eggshells : Taking Your Life Back When Someone You Care About Has Borderline Personality Disorder.* New harbinger Publications, Inc.: Oakland.

McKay, Mathew., et al. (1983). *How to Communicate: The Ultimate Guide to Improving Your Personal and Professional Relationships.* MJF Books: New York.

McTaggart, Lynne. (2002). *The Field: The Quest for the Secret Force of the Universe.* HarperCollins: New York.

Meehan, Mary, et al. (1997). *The Future Ain't What It Use To Be.* Penguin Putnam Inc.: New York.

Miller, William and Stephen Rollnick. (2002). *Motivational Interviewing: Preparing People for Change.* (Second edition). The Guilford Press: New York.

Morgan, Gareth. (1966). *Images of Organizations.* Sage Publications: Newborn Park.

Moss, Leonard. (1981). *Management Stress.* Addison-Wesley Publishing Co.

Murphy, Emmett C. (1996). *Leadership IQ: A Personal Development Process Based on a Scientific Study of a New Generation Of Leaders.* John Wiley and Sons: New York.

Myss, Carolyn. (1996). *Anatomy of the Spirit: The Seven Stages of Power and Healing.* Harmony Books: New York.

Myss, Carolyn. (2001). *Sacred Contracts: Awakening Your Divine Potential.* Sounds True: Boulder CO.

Naisbitt, John. And Patricia Aburdene (1990). *Megatrends 2000: Ten New Directions for the 1990's.* William Morrow And Co., Inc.: New York.

Neave, Henry R. (1991). *The Deming Dimension.* SPC Press, Inc.: Knoxville, Tenn.

Oakley, Ed and Doug Krug. (1991). *Enlightened Leadership: Getting to the Heart Of Change.* Fireside: New York.

Ouchi, William. (1981). *Theory Z: How American Business Can Meet the Japanese Challenge.* Addison-Wesley: Menlo Park, Calif.

Papadopoulos, Renos K. And Graham S. Saayman. (Eds.). (1991). *Jung In Modern Perspective: The Master And His Legacy.* Unity Press: Australia.

Peck, M. Scott (1987). *The Different Drum: Community-Making and Peace.* Simon and Schuster: New York.

Peck, M. Scott. (1983). *People of the Lie: The Hope for Healing Human Evil.* Simon and Schuster, Inc.: New York.

Peck, M. Scott. (1993). *A World Waiting To Be Born: Civility Rediscovered.* Bantam Books: New York.

Peppers, Don and Martha Rogers. (1996). *The One To One Future: Building Relationships One Customer At A Time.* Currency: New York.

Peppers, Don and Martha Rogers. (1997). *Enterprise One To One: Tools for Competing in the Interactive Age.* Currency: New York.

Peters, Tom. (1988). *Thriving On Chaos: Handbook For A Management Revolution.* Alfred A. Knopf: New York.

Peters, Tom. (1994). *The Pursuit Of Wow: Every Person's Guide to Topsy-Turvy Times.* Random House, Inc.: New York.

Petrock. Frank. (1990). Five Stages Of Team Development. *Executive Excellence. 7* (6), 9–10.

Popcorn, Faith. (1991). *The Popcorn Report: Faith Popcorn on the Future of Your Company, Your World, Your Life. Doubleday Currency:* New York.

Ritzer, George. (2000). *The Mcdonaldization Of Society.* Pine Forge Press: Thousand Oaks.

Robbins, Stephen P. (1988). *Management.* (Second Ed.) Prentice Hall: New Jersey.

Roberts, Wess. (1990). *Leadership Secrets of Attila the Hun.* Warner Books. New York.

Rodale, Jerome I. (1978). *The Synonym Finder: Special Deluxe Edition.* Rodale Press: Emmaus, Pa.

Rosen, Robert with Lisa Berger. (1991). *The Healthy Company: Eight Strategies to Develop People, Productivity and Profits.* Jeremy P. Tarcher/Perigree: New York.

Rosen, Robert. (1986). *Healthy Companies: A Human Resource Approach (AMA Management Briefing).* AMA Membership Publications Division, AMA, NY.

Rossi, Ernest L. (1993). *The Psychobiology of Mind-Body Healing.* Revised edition. W. W. Norton and Company, Inc.: New York.

Rubin, Harriet. (1997). *The Princessa: Machiavelli for Women.* Currency: New York.

Rubin, Lillian B. (1976). *Worlds of Pain: Life in the Working-Class Family.* Basic Books, Inc., Publishers: New York.

Rubin, Lillian. B. (1994). *Families on the Fault Line: America's Working Class Speaks About the Family, the Economy, Race and Ethnicity.* Harper Perennial: New York.

Ruche, K.E. (n.d.) Influencing performance in manufacturing work systems: An examination of causal relationships of organizational structures and situational workplace variables on proactive management behavior. DIA, 54(07).

Rusk, Tom. (1993). *The Power of Ethical Persuasion: From Conflict to Partnership at Work and In Private Life.* Penguin Books: New York.

Ryan, Kathleen D. and Daniel K. Oestreich. (1991). *Driving Fear Out of the Workplace: How to Overcome the Invisible Barriers to Quality, Productivity, and Innovation.* Jossey-Bass: San Francisco.

Salter, Anna, C. (2003). *Predators: Pedophiles, Rapists, and Other Sex Offenders. Who they Are, How They Operate, and How We Can Protect Ourselves and Our Children.* Basic Books: New York.

Safari, William. (1993). *Safari's New Political Dictionary: The Definitive Guide to the New Language of Politics.* Random House: New York.

Samuels, Aandrew, et al. (1993). *A Critical Dictionary of Jungian Analysis.* Routledge and Kegan Paul LTD: New York.

Schellardt, Timothy D. (1996, August 1). Are Layoffs Moral? One Firm's Answer: You Ask, We'll Sue. *The Wall Street Journal.*

Schmidt, John E. (1993). Transformational Leadership: The Relationship Between Consciousness, Values and Skills (Leadership). *DIA, 54(11A), 4057.*

Senge, Peter. (1990). *The Fifth Discipline.* Doubleday: New York.

Sheehy, Gail. (1995). *New Passages: Mapping Your Life Across Time.* Random House, Inc.: New York.

Simons, George F., et al. (1993). *Transcultural Leadership: Empowering the Diverse Workforce.* Gulf Publishing Company: Houston.

Skinner, Burrhus F. (1965). *Science and Human Behavior*. Free Press: New York.

Slusser, Gerald H. (1986). *From Jung to Jesus: Myth and Consciousness in the New Testament*. John Knox Press: Atlanta.

Storey, John. (1994). *Cultural Theory and Popular Culture: A Reader*. Harvester/Wheatsheaf: New York.

Sundstrom, E., DeMeuse, K. P. and Futrell, D. (1990). Work Teams. *American Psychologist*. 120–133.

Sztompka, Piotr. (1993). *The Sociology of Social Change*. Blackwell, Oxford U.K. and Cambridge U.S.A.

Terkel, Studs. (1986). *Hard Times: An Oral History of the Great Depression*. Pantheon Books: New York.

Terkel, Studs. (1995). Coming of Age: The Story of Our Century By Those Who've Lived It. The New Press: New York.

Terry, Robert. W. (1993). *Authentic Leadership: Courage in Action*. Jossey-Bass: San Francisco.

The New York Times. (1996). Special Report: The Downsizing of America. Millions of Americans are Losing Good Jobs. This Is Their Story. Expanded to include additional reporting and reader responses to the extraordinary series by the reporters of *The New York Times*.

Torres, Cresencio and Jerry Spiegel. (1990). *Self-Directed Work Teams: A Primer*. Pfeiffer and Co.: San Diego.

Tuckman, Bruce. W. (1965). Developmental Sequence in Small Groups. *Psychological Bulletin*.

Ury, William. (1991). *Getting Past No: Negotiating With Difficult People*. Bantam Doubleday Dell: New York.

Walding, Dana M. (1994). Spirituality and Leadership. *DIA*, *55* (7A), 1783.

Wall, Bob, et al. (1992). *The Visionary Leader: From Mission Statement to A Thriving Organization, Here's Your Blueprint for Building an Inspired Cohesive, Customer-Oriented Team*. Prima: Rocklin, Calif.

Walton, Clarence C. (1988). *The Moral Manager*. Harper Business: New York.

Ward, Lewis B. (1965). "The Ethics of Executive Selection," *Harvard Business Review*, 43 (2), 6–28.

Watson, Charles E. (1999). *What Smart People Do When Dumb Things Happen At Work : Tips for Solving Real-World Work Problems*. Barnes Noble Books: New York.

Watts, Duncan J. (2003) *Six Degrees: The Science of a Connected Age*. W. W. Norton and Company: New York.

Watzlawick, Paul. (1984). *The Invented Reality: How Do We Know What We Believe We Know? (Contributions To Constructivism)*. W.W. Norton and Company.

Weber, Max. (1995). *The Protestant Ethic and the Spirit of Capitalism*. Translated by T. Parsons. Introduction by A. Gibbens, Fellow of King's College, Cambridge. Routledge: New York.

Weisbord, Marvin R. (1987). *Productive Workplaces: Organizing and Managing for Dignity, Meaning, and Community*. Jossey-Bass: San Francisco.

West, Cornel. (1991). *Race Matters*. Beacon Press: Boston.

Wheatley, Margaret J. (1992). *Leadership and The New Science: Learning About Organization from an Orderly Universe*. Berrett-Koehler: San Francisco.

Wheatley, Margaret. J. and Myron Kellner-Rogers. (1996). *A Simpler Way*. Berrett-Koehler: San Francisco.

Wiley, Ralph. (1991). *Why Black People Tend to Shout: Cold Facts and Wry Views From a Black Man's World*. Penguin Books: New York.

Wolinsky, Stephen. (1993). *Quantum Consciousness: The Guide to Experiencing Quantum Psychology*. Bramble Books: Northfork, Conn.

Wolinsky, Stephen. (1999a). *The Way of The Human: Volume I Developing Multi-Dimensional Awareness. The Quantum Psychology Notebooks* (Special section: Trances people live revised). Quantum Institute: Capitola, Cali.

Wolinsky, Stephen. (1999b). *The Way Of The Human: Volume II The False Core And The False Self. The Quantum Psychology Notebooks*. Quantum Institute: Capitola, California.

Wolinsky, Stephen. (1999c). *The Way Of The Human: Volume III Beyond Quantum Psychology: The Quantum Psychology Notebooks*. (Special section: Trances people live revised) Quantum Institute: Capitola, California.

Yankelovich, Daniel. (1981). *New Rules: Searching for Self-Fulfillment in a World Turned Upside Down*. Random House: New York.

Yukl, Gary. A. (1981). *Leadership in Organizations*. Prentice Hall: Enlewood Cliffs, N.J.

CPSIA information can be obtained at www.ICGtesting.com
Printed in the USA
LVOW08s0721170814

399509LV00002B/621/P